THE ARENA

Mark Ewald
2341 Rockwell Ct.
Kettering, OH 45420

marktewald@gmail.com

979-8-9859107-0-4

THE
ARENA
STAND TALL

Mark T. Ewald

**TRUE STORIES FROM THE COMPETITIVE
ARENA OF HUMAN EXPERIENCE**

Eternal thanks to my amazing and resilient wife, Diane, who has supported my chase of the coaching journey and enabled me to experience all the amazing memories along the way. You have given me so much!

To my beloved children, Nick, Jackie, and Luke: I love you and am so proud of you. You have supported my passion for coaching and made many sacrifices along the way.

To my family, and especially my sister, Karla, who always listened to the ups and downs.

To my late mother, Regina, who always understood why I coached and wanted to hear all the details.

And to all my players, coaches, and other folks I have been blessed to meet along the way. A huge thank you to all those who have shared their stories of inspiration, pain, and perseverance to make this book a reality.

YOU NEVER THROW WITH ME!

I remember it like it was last fall. But it was 48 years ago. I was sitting in the back seat of my 6th-grade football coach's paneled station wagon. He was driving me and my twin brother, Mike, to practice when someone near the open window said "Did you hear about Ewald's dad?" Not sure why it did not register with me at the time. It may have been Coach's immediate distraction, or him talking about the big championship game that coming Sunday that Mike and I would be playing for Visitation BVM (Blessed Virgin Mother), just outside of Philadelphia. Our fight song was *When the Saints Come Marching In*.... Being Friday and two days before the championship struggle, we had work to do to get ready to battle our Catholic school rival for the 6th-grade Title for 1972.

Coach Basale was a Vietnam vet who coached from a wheelchair; having lost a leg in the war, he was unable to walk because of injuries sustained in battle. Undeterred by the inconvenience of paralysis, he would chase us around in his silver wheelchair with his white-hot grey hair, a whistle clinched in his teeth, the veins bulging in his neck.

It was like a slow-motion nightmare movie that was beginning shortly after Coach drove us home and we pulled into a driveway full of cars. We were surprised by the company, since we thought Mom and Dad were in NY at a work convention. When we got to the door there was a priest and our uncles, Ted and Val, from our parents' family back in Ohio, along with other assorted friends and my father's coworkers: many strangers dressed in black. Very naive about the world and life, I thought we were having a party. The memory is a little foggy, but all I remember was Mom explaining to us that Dad had a heart attack and went to heaven. In shock and total disbelief, I could not transmit this unreal information to my young brain, so instead I ran. Out the front door I ran, away from this impossible twist in our lives. I just ran and cried as I sprinted to our camp a few fields away from our house in Audubon, PA.

The horror of my smart-ass comments – my last words to my father a few days earlier, "You never throw with me!" haunted me and made feel sick to my stomach. My father, Carl Earl Ewald, 46 years young, was in bed with flu-like symptoms during that last conversation. Obviously, he had something serious going on leading up to the massive heart attack he would have a few days later.

He had just overseen the Allstate Insurance Company's sales convention at the Waldorf Astoria in Manhattan. He had just taken a carriage ride with my mother in Central Park. They were in the Presidential Suite when his heart gave out. He was soon to be named the President of Allstate Insurance; that never materialized. The last time we spoke, he was too ill to go outside and toss the ball with me. If only I could go back in time and take the words back and just hug him. I was scared to sleep that night, and felt even worse that he was gone because of my comments and because of our last interaction.

It seemed in that moment that my life and football became entwined.

Mike and I played that Sunday in the title game because Dad would have wanted us to. I do not remember much about the game except that they gave me a big trophy as MVP. I remember crying in my uncle's arms and them saying how proud Dad was of us. The MVP was not a runaway or really deserved in a 0-0 defensive struggle. I may have had a couple of TFL's, and a 30-yard run, but got the big trophy out of sympathy most likely. Nevertheless, my brother Mike's glum face in the photo on our front porch was a combination of the sadness of losing our beloved father and me getting a gaudy trophy instead of him. Dad would have been proud of our competitive natures, even in the specter of sadness and a soon-to-be changed life.

My entire life, any time my kids or anyone else asked me to throw, I have jumped at the chance, I suppose deep down to wipe away my guilt and to honor my Dad. I know you would have thrown with me if you felt better, Dad! I'm so sorry those were my last words to you, and I miss you and love you!

MTE

ATTACK AND COMPETE!

Success is based on hard work. Period. People talk about talent and ability, but I will take hard work every time. Success, in anything, just does not happen. Work, preparation, and time determine it.

During the summer before my senior year at Wittenberg, I wrecked a four-wheeler and lacerated my spleen in three places. Needless to say, I was not able to play football that season. I remember vividly the doctor saying matter of factly, "No more football for you." I knew he meant for the upcoming season, but did he mean forever?

The healing process was long and arduous, but I remember the feeling when I was finally cleared to start working out again. It was great. I then began the thought process of deciding whether to return for a fifth year and play football. I was finished with school, but still had one more year of eligibility. I decided to come back and play, but I knew it would be tough to get back to the physical shape and conditioning level I was at before the injury. Hard work wins!

Slowly but steadily, I got back into shape and was probably in the best shape of my life. Our season got off to a rough start, and I started questioning my decision to return. Is this worth it, I asked myself repeatedly. I knew myself and my teammates worked way too hard for the season to be going in the direction it was. We banded together through adversity, turned things around, and won the conference.

The team was talented, but more importantly to me, it had some average guys willing to bust their tails for a common goal. I made a great decision!

Attack and Compete!

ADAM HEWITT

NOT JUST A T-SHIRT

As an assistant at Hamilton High School under Jim Place, I experienced one of my greatest moments as a coach. My first fall at Hamilton in 2007, there was a senior named Todd Dell.

Todd was the type of kid you could just tell did not have a whole lot going for him. He was not a very talented or skilled football player either.

Brad Watkins (the other offensive line coach) and I decided that year to create an "Offensive Lineman of the Day" t-shirt for our August camp. We would give one out every day to the offensive lineman we felt had worked the hardest and improved the most. And let me tell you, we had some talented guys on the offensive line. Phil Manley, who went to Toledo and was on the Falcons roster, for one. We had other very talented linemen as well. As fall camp progressed, Todd was really struggling, but he just worked his ass off every day.

I think it was his first year playing football. It was easy to see that he would most likely never be able to play for us that season, with all the talented guys we had, but we coached the hell out of Todd every day and he kept improving every day. His persistence and work ethic after an extremely tough practice convinced us he deserved that day's "Lineman of the Day" t-shirt. We always called the guys up after the last practice of the day and handed out the t-shirt. When we announced Todd, he was a wobbly and sweaty mess from getting his teeth kicked in by the other hogs. After we announced it to the guys, Todd breaks down and starts crying, right there on the field. Brad and I were a bit shocked at first and did not really know how to react. We started reassuring him that he was the player of the day because he earned it. He was overjoyed and beaming with pride. It was obvious he had never been recognized like this before. The whole scene reinforced and amplified the key role coaches and positive reinforcement can have on our young people. Not sure where Todd is these days, but I am convinced he is a more confident individual for being a part of the Hogs and Hamilton Football Program.

And that is what it's all about!

ANONYMOUS

DIRTY 30

As I entered my first year as head football coach, I was excited, energized, and highly motivated by the fear of failure. I had been hired by the high school I had graduated from, and many people in that community knew me and my family. After securing the position, I began to see that there would be significant challenges. During the spring prior to my hiring (I was hired in late May), our school district had decided to implement a 2.0 academic participation standard for athletes.

As you can imagine, there were students who did not believe the district was serious about these standards. There were also many students who just did not take their studies seriously. In both cases the student athletes found themselves ineligible for the fall season – my debut season. I also quickly learned that the weightlifting standards were minimal in the past. The weight room was one flat bench and six Universal stations on the balcony of the gym. As if these two factors were not enough for me to rethink my decision to take the job, at my first team meeting there were only 30 players in attendance. We began the season with 30, and as it would turn out, ended with 30 players.

In that meeting, I'm sure my message was the same as thousands of other coaches' messages to their teams on the very first day. However, I remember talking with my assistant coaches and we all concurred that we needed to be brutally honest with the team about expectations for the upcoming season. I talked to them about how we were not expected to do well that season, and that preseason newspaper prognostications had us finishing near the bottom, if not at the bottom, of the league. I told them it was important that everyone in that room, coaches and players, needed to believe otherwise. Then I gave them the speech that every coach gives about each player having a role to play on the team, and about playing that role to the best of their ability. You know the speech: "It's going to take all of us!" We ended the meeting with the players adopting a nickname for the team. They wanted to call themselves the "Dirty Thirty", a kind of spin-off of the "Dirty Dozen" movie.

As is the case on any team, we had our best player, and our worst player, "Robert" was the worst player on the team. He was a guard, with no speed, no size, and no athletic ability. Our first game that season was an away game. It was against an opponent that historically finished somewhere in the middle of the pack, as far as league play was concerned. In our area the local newspaper was (and still is) the *Dayton Daily News*. Each week during the high school football season, they would have 4 or 5 sports reporters and/or local celebrities make predictions on who would win the games in the area. We were picked to lose that opening night by all those doing the prognosticating.

Aside from the fact that this was my first game as the head coach of my alma mater, the game was a highly stressful game from a coaching standpoint. We played the game in our end of the field the entire game. We could never get field position flipped. The game was 0 to 0 late in the 3rd quarter and our opponent was driving. I was walking down the sideline to talk to my defensive coordinator when I saw our team doctor working intensely on one of our players who was lying on the ground on his back. As I got closer and saw the player's face, I realized it was Robert. The next part of this story I'm not proud of. My first thought was not "Is Robert OK?". I exploded! Who put Robert in the game? Who put the 30th guy of the "Dirty 30" in the game with the game on the line, tied 0-0? At this point I had arrived where my defensive coordinator was standing and unloaded on him. "Did you put Robert in the game?" He exploded in kind and yelled at me, "No, did you put him in the game?" An immediate and intense interrogation began of all assistant coaches, including those in the press box, on our headphones. No one was accepting responsibility for putting Robert in the game. I was adamant about getting to the bottom of this. I was furious! This went on for several minutes. At some point, having heard the discord among coaches, the team doctor approached me. "Coach Turner," he said, "no one put Robert in the game." As it turned out, Robert was doing what we talked about way back in the first meeting during camp in August. Robert was playing his role to the best of his ability. He had been cheering and yelling and supporting his team. He had gotten so animated that he hyperventilated and collapsed, passing out on the sideline.

We ended up winning that game 7-0. Robert and the rest of the "Dirty 30" finished the season at 7-3 and tied for the league championship. It was the first championship in over a decade for our high school. As I look back on my 40-year coaching career, this is one of the stories I remember most. I remember it because it taught me some valuable coaching lessons. Every player is important, and every play can contribute in some way. Each time a coach speaks someone is listening, and taking what is said to heart. I never took the "playing your role" speech or the concept of having a role to play lightly after that season. The unfortunate ending to this story is that Robert lost his life in his early 30s to illness. It's my understanding that he led his short life the same way he supported his teammates in that first game, with great enthusiasm, playing his role to the best of his ability. He was a good, supportive friend to many of the players on his team and after high school. For me, as his coach, I learned from Robert some valuable life and coaching lessons that I have continued to use and continue to pass on to others.

COACH CRAIG TURNER

JUST WAITING ON THE BUS

The game of football has taken me down some roads I never would have expected. James took me down one of those roads. James was an average player with a great attitude. He always brought some juice to practice and had a positive vibe. Never heard him complain or mope around. Really a testament to what kind of a young man he was and what he overcame every day.

He was a sophomore when I noticed him at the bus station the first time. I started going by the bus stop that fall because my wife, Jill, and I had just built our first house three miles east of school. So I noticed him standing at the station that took him to the river's edge area, west of town. The tougher part of Memphis. I would wave and every few days I noticed him. I asked him why he was at the station so often and he said his parents where working. I had never met them, which is a lesson I learned about coaching that year: Take the time to sit with each family!

James's older brother, Sam, was the one who would pick him up and was the only family member I ever saw. As a coach you are busy preparing and sometimes you miss things that make a difference in your guys' lives. I missed his real family dynamic. I would often want to ask him if he wanted a ride, but with the modern rules of disallowing just one kid without another adult in the car, offering a ride was difficult. I get it; but one day it was pouring buckets of rain. The bus stop in the back of the stadium that went toward the river's edge had no canopy; it was just a pole with a sign on it. He looked like a wet cat as my wipers slapped my window. He was holding his equipment bag over his head. I pulled up and I said, "James get in the back -- I will run you by your place." He hesitated and said, "Thanks coach, but bus should be here soon." I persisted and he begrudgingly got in. We had small talk about his role as a scout defensive player. As we neared the neighborhood, I was taken aback by the poverty and run-down houses.

He had me pull in front of one of the nicer houses. He said, "Thanks coach, see you tomorrow," cheerfully and jumped out. I pulled to the end of the street and was turning back towards the highway, away from this sad area James lived in. It made me think. I stopped at the stop sign and could see him through the rain in my mirror. I was surprised to see him stand there and start walking back the other way. He went out of sight, so I turned right and went down an alley behind several houses. You could barely get down the alley because of trash and old cars parked behind garages, or what was left of them. It had started raining more heavily, but I saw James get into a van at the end of the alley. I was really perplexed. I knew it was not a drivable vehicle because it had a torn blue tarp flapping out the back and its tires were pretty much flat. I backed up, drove around the block, and pulled back up the alley where the van was. It was obvious the house it was parked behind was unlivable. There was a gaping hole in the roof and it was just a mess: broken windows, etc. I sat there a minute and felt sick to my stomach that a young player on our team lived here. I felt sad and ashamed. Pretty sad that I was worried about how the hell I felt.

I got out of the car and went up to the side of the van. I sneaked around the side and looked inside. There was James with a towel over his head. There was a single light bulb hanging from the ceiling. I could see a red extension cord out a rusted hole above the bumper. I was getting sick to my stomach and my heart was racing. I felt terrible, small, selfish!

I wasn't sure what to do – I knocked on the back door. I later thought about that and shook my head. Like it was his front door? Wow! I could hear movement as the van moved. No answer. I knew he saw my car. After a few minutes, I said, "James, it's Coach -- let's talk, open the door." The door opened and the look of horror and sadness in his eyes I will never forget. Ever!

I don't exactly remember what I first said or what he said. But he was pissed. He asked what I was thinking, spying on him, coming onto his street. I was on the defensive. I got a few words in and asked where his parents were and what was he doing? He started crying and slammed the rusty back doors. I stood there in dismay. My phone was ringing, and Jill was probably wondering where I was. I picked up and said I would be home later. Just said I was with a player. She said, "Okay...?!"

I stood there and just wanted to take him away. I blurted out: let's go get a burger. Grab your coat, let's go, I'm hungry. He yelled back: no thanks! I stood my ground and said I was not leaving. He finally opened the door and said "okay." His opening that door changed both of our lives forever.

I could waste pages on the ups and downs of this new challenge in my life and in my family. But asking him to get in that day was one of the best decisions of my life. After a big cheeseburger and some vegetable soup I got James to talk. But only after I had promised not to turn him in. His mom and dad had been in and out of his life the last few years because of drugs and a rough life — as he put it. Sam, his brother, was working in a factory but got mixed up with some guys in the corner-drug game.

He told me he had been getting by fine. He said he was going to do better. He was adamant that I did not get him in trouble. I went to the bathroom and I got sick. Our conversation was just too much. As I washed my face and looked into the mirror, I was committed to making this right for James! I came back to the table with an attitude that would win him over. I told him to get some pie. He laughed and said okay. As he finished, I told him he was going home with me and that we would work on making things better. Amazingly, he initially said no and that he was fine. He said that he was doing well in school. I was indeed stunned later, as I learned more about him, that he was a solid student despite his environment. The human spirit is amazing!

There is so much more to tell, but there is not enough paper or time. I never realized how my life (and my beloved wife's) would change that day, and still don't 13 years later. I would like to say it was easy and we all lived happily ever after. But that isn't life. It has been a difficult, exhausting, enriching struggle. But there are no regrets! I mean that from the deepest part of my being.

We became partial guardians to James, and we love him like our own son. He battled more days than not. He wanted his family to heal but they just did not. His brother went the wrong way and is now incarcerated. James wants a relationship with him and is trying so hard. James is still winning every day! There have been a ton of tough days, but he persevered. James played football and also played basketball in high school. As a coach and a father figure, I am amazed by and so proud of James. He became a mentor to many young people. He doesn't like his story being told too often, thus I offer limited details, like names, dates, school, etc.

But he is a testament to overcoming obstacles and thriving. James, to me, is a lesson in perseverance, and to anyone who is down and feeling out: it's never as bad as it seems! James is a medical technician after completing a community college program. He is a winner in so many ways. I am so grateful to have stopped that day at the bus stop and the trip that road has taken me!

Thanks, James.

JWK

CROSSROADS
— COMPETITOR FROM THE FIELD TO BOARDROOM —

I was at a crossroads in my life. I could continue to work for my employer of 8 years and make a great living; but I did not believe in the product solutions my firm provided our clients.

OR I could leave my employer and start my own business under the umbrella of another firm with better product solutions, but knowing the transition of clients would be a long, arduous process. When I finally made the decision to leave my employer and start my own business at another firm, I was newly married and my wife was not pregnant. Two weeks after I made the decision, guess what: the wife was pregnant!

I worked 93 days straight after making the decision to transfer companies. Many clients came with me to the new firm, several stayed, and there was still a good quantity that were undecided. Long story short, my ex-employer and new employer entered into an arbitration: I could not reach out to previous clients if they had not transitioned to my new employer for the next 12 months. There was still much work to do and still many people to get in touch with, but now I was unable to reach out to them. At my previous employer, I was used to prospects walking in the door, but at my new employer there were no warm hand-offs by the firm. Rather, it was "go find your own new clients." At that moment I had a decent base but I was not where I was before, and my pipeline of new prospects was no longer available. I thought I had played this out in my mind before, but the reality was much harder; and I was mentally exhausted from working 80 hours a week for several months.

I had many sleepless nights, suffered panic attacks, and was depressed. I was my own worst enemy. I questioned myself: why would you leave an easy job that paid you well and was fairly stress-free? Now you have a pregnant wife and have created self-induced uncertainty. I relentlessly beat myself up. In reflecting, I now understand that sleep is vital to your health. I can go one or two days with very little sleep, but when you string out multiple days of sleeplessness, then it can negatively affect one's mental state and perspective.

Eventually, I reached out to God. I prayed: "I can't do this on my own and I need your help." This was hard for me because I was/am a control freak. I had always gone to church but was a lukewarm Christian, aka, a "catch you on Sunday morning" church attender.

I broke down the complexity of the transition into a sequence I repeated to myself: 1. Have faith in God, 2. Do the best that you can for those you serve (my clients), 3. I will not fail my family … especially not my unborn baby, Aljancic. I started reading Scripture daily and listening to church sermons online during my commutes, but I still was not "all in" for God. I still wanted to be in control. One morning, I woke up at 4am and decided to get a jump start on work. It was a morning after several bad nights of sleep. I was driving downtown and mentally I was beat up...depressed. It was winter, and the sermon I was listening to on this drive was about how the ancient Greeks viewed time: "chronos" and "kairos." Chronos measures time in minutes, hours, days, etc. Kairos measures "special moments or opportunistic moments" that strike you in life. As the pastor was discussing "kairos moments," I turned left off the highway toward my office. Half a mile ahead of me was the giant 47-floor LeVeque Tower, and every room's light was turned off EXCEPT the lit rooms that formed a large lighted cross. I wept in my car as I drove. It was my personal kairos moment. God showed me a sign that He was with me. That moment renewed my faith and gave me strength to continue to grind out 80-hour weeks for several more months, and I learned how to earn new clients via networking and cold calling.

Without that difficult time in my life, I would not be as close to God as I am today, and I would not have a business that is much larger and more fulfilling than my previous job. Bottom line is that having faith and outworking your competition will put anyone in the position they want to be in. 99% of jobs do not require elite intelligence; rather, if one grinds harder and works well with others, they will find themselves at the top of their peer class in whatever profession they choose. There are people much smarter than I that will never have a successful business because they are not willing to put in the work. It's as simple as saying "SUCCESSFUL people do the things daily that UNSUCCESSFUL people are not willing to do." We are in a world full of "mainstream media" and "punch the clock" individuals. Those that have faith in God have great perspective, and those that outwork their peers/competition "make their own luck." I've come to learn that life isn't fair, and EVERYONE has challenges. Life isn't about giving handouts, but when a person continuously works harder than the competition, positive outcomes are much more likely and are more frequent. We face choices daily. We can CHOOSE to give the best of our ability or we can CHOOSE to go through the motions. Outcomes have direct correlation with work ethic.

I CHOOSE to have faith, do the best I can for those I serve, and outwork my competition. That is my simple recipe.

M.A.

THE DOME

The concept of "The Dome" is one of the cornerstones of my program. Imagine a clear, tinted dome that covers the entire football field from sideline to sideline and end line to end line. Inside this dome is a perfect world. There is no prejudice, no bigotry, no rich, or poor, no Catholic, Protestant, Jewish, Muslim, Buddhist, no white, black, brown, yellow, no Italian, Mexican, Irish, African. Inside the dome, it does not matter who your mom and dad are or which neighborhood you live in. You control your destiny in the dome. Disrespect is never allowed. If you do not like someone who is different from you (race, religion, culture), we will find someone from that group to knock you down. Discipline is a must. If you are told to put your toes on the line, you put them on the line, not 6 inches over the line or 6 inches behind the line. You are judged on how you act and the respect you earn. It is a perfect world, and you should look forward to coming into the dome every day. If you act like a man, you will be treated like a man.

When presenting the dome concept to the players, I ask two players to go outside the dome. I tell them that they are in the outside world, where there is prejudice, bigotry, laziness, cheating, etc. The real world has all these bad things. I then bring the players back into the dome, and the entire team cheers for them because they are coming back into a perfect world.

I challenge my players to live their entire lives in the dome.

It was in my first few months as the head coach of the "Middletown Middies," and the players had not yet heard the story of the "Middie Dome". Someone came to my office and said, "Two of the best senior players are going to fight." One was a big, mean white guy, the other a short, really tough black guy. I asked them, "What's up?" They proceeded to tell me their stories. After a long time, I said, "Wait a minute, is this racial?" They both said yes, and I responded, "Why didn't you tell me that 10 minutes ago? It would have made this whole thing easy. You are both cut, I will not coach a team that has racial prejudice, and the way to make sure that happens is to cut both of you." They were shocked and made sure that I knew they were two of the best players. I told them to leave and that I was going to call our school safety officer and ask him to be on the lookout at the park, because "you two were probably going to be showing up". About 15 minutes later, I heard a knock on the door, and it was the two players. The said they had misunderstood what I meant by racial and that they didn't feel that way. I told them about the dome and that since I had not told them about the dome before, I would take them back, but they had to have their lockers next to each other, sit on the bus next to each other, eat next to each other at pregame meals, and if I ever sensed any disrespect, they were gone. They agreed, and I am sure you know the result. They became good friends and even today speak fondly of each other.

COACH JIM PLACE

PUT ME IN, COACH! NO PROBLEM!

Jeff Bonner was an Oakwood graduate of the Class of 2004.

At 5'9" and 175 lbs his senior year, he was a dime a dozen in terms of how he was measured... Until you measured his heart.

My story about Jeff goes back to his freshman year. He was 150 lbs back then, and quiet, but had a competitive edge. His job was to be the backup QB for a junior who was a stud. His marching orders were to be attentive during practice in case something happened to the starter.

Now usually when you give that message to a normal freshman it is lip service, and you find out later when called upon they were not locking in too well. He probably knows two plays and they look sloppy at that. Well, as you can guess, his time came with 40 seconds left in a game vs. the Carlisle Indians in the fall of 2000. Our starter broke his leg with us down by 6 and the ball on the 37 yd line going in. I had no time-outs left and called a play "Rocket 600 Z Post". Our little freshman QB goes into the game and throws a TD in the back of the end zone. Unfortunately, one of our wings on the PAT unit failed to step down and we ended up in overtime.

I was concerned, considering this was a kid with one snap of experience. However, I was astonished when I asked him, "How do you feel about what I can call?" He told me, "Coach, I know all of your stuff; I have been watching all season like you told me."

In the next series from the 20 yd line after our defense had held, I call a boot pass, a counter, and a draw for a touchdown. If you were watching the game, you would have thought he had been doing it all year.

He went on to have a Hall of Fame career as a football and basketball player at Oakwood. I was lucky enough to coach him for 36 football games and 67 basketball games.

Every season I coach — I look for the Jeff Bonners for that season. I have yet to find anyone close. He was never late to one meeting. As a matter of fact, he was always 20 minutes early for the 4 years of football and basketball that I coached him.

I tell the Jeff Bonner story to every team I coach, waiting for someone to get it. Waiting for some young man to figure out what it means to be coachable, humble, competitive, driven, accountable, and responsible, to name a few attributes.

We all want that kid who listens to everything we say and can execute the plan. I have had it once.

In closing, I went to Jeff's wedding this past summer, nine years after I coached him in his last game. Listening to others talk about Jeff Bonner the adult, and now the husband, verified that others have discovered what I have always known about him. He is everything I want my eight-year-old to be. Trust me, I tell my son the Jeff Bonner story every chance I get.

By the way, Jeff is a pediatrician. Not bad for a 5'9", 150 lb "frosh"!

PAUL STONE

WHAT IT MEANS TO BE A FIREBIRD

Sometimes 12 years of coaching seems like two, and other times it feels like I have been doing it for 25. Either way, these years of coaching have been a true blessing and the most rewarding times of my life. The relationships built, the emotions experienced, and the memories stored are things that have left a deep imprint on me as a coach, a son, a husband, and a father of two daughters. The story I want to share is one about Michael Klenk.

Michael was a 6'0" tall, slender backup QB with a smile that would light up a stadium. From an outsider's point of view, he was a typical high school athlete who played football and baseball; however, nothing could be further from the truth. Michael was born with cystic fibrosis — the destructive lung disease that makes doing the most "normal" daily task very difficult. As we all know, being a high school football player is very physically demanding: strength training, pushing sleds on the field, tackling dummies, multiple sprints, and running everywhere during a practice and game. For most players these demands are tough, but it's part of the routine: hop out of bed, grab a quick bite to eat, maybe a Gatorade, and get to practice and workouts. And to be a good player, you must repeat this process every day.

That routine was not that easy for Michael. Each morning he had to wake up much earlier than all teammates to prepare his body for the typical "grind". This process entailed an intense breathing treatment to help him clear out his lungs so he could make it through each day's practices and workouts. Unless Michael or someone close to him told you, you would never know what he was dealing with or what he had to endure to be a varsity athlete. Most people in Michael's situation would ask "why me?" or think "I am tired of doing all this just to play a sport." That was not in his DNA. He loved his teammates, and he loved being a contributing member of his team. He was the type of player that did everything a coach asked and then a little more.

He was a leader by example, and players and students followed his lead. He understood what it took to be a champion, an elite teammate on the field and off. He did what was necessary. Whether it was running extra sprints or running scout team QB, he loved it and relished his role; he did it with unbridled enthusiasm. Michael had talent but was not the star, never got a ton of attention, but that never mattered to him. What mattered was helping his team get better every day and enjoying everything about the daily grind and process.

After his graduation from high school, his lungs began to fail and he ended up requiring a lung transplant. The surgery at first seem to go well, but eventually, in 2008, his body could not handle the strain and couldn't fight it any longer, and he passed away. His body failed but not his memory or spirit. What Michael left us was a clear picture of what a true "Firebird" epitomizes, and what it meant to bleed blue and silver. We often talk about him and the type of person/player he was around our field house. During Michael's senior year we created an award in his name to celebrate and recognize the attributes of a great teammate, leader, and football family member, the kind we coaches strive to have in our program. Family is a key word in Michael's life and his mother, father, brother, and sister supported, pushed, and loved him unconditionally. They, along with Michael, showed us all how to live life, be it way too short for Michael.

The plaque we all touch as we take the field on Friday nights. It reads: *This award was established in 2005 to honor a Fairmont football player who, for four years, has chosen to exemplify the qualities and characteristics that embody what it means to be a Firebird. These qualities are: Selflessness, Commitment, Dedication, & Loyalty.*

Thank you and God bless you, Michael, and your family!

COACH ANDY ARACARI

FAMILY FIRST

To have longevity in coaching, one must be supported by a great family. It must be a family-driven process. When I was a young coach (had been coaching for about 10 years), I landed the head coaching job at Boca Raton High School in Florida. I believed that to be a good coach, you had to out-work your opponent by burning the candle at both ends, no matter what was going on both in season and out of season. Of course, anyone with a family would know that many family times were lost, and I could never get those times back. I had preached "Faith, Family, and Football" to our players from day one. I wanted our players to be great players, but equally as important I wanted them to be great men, great husbands, and great dads. That is why I got into coaching. Well, I was blessed with two of the best daughters a man could have and a coach's wife that was extremely supportive. They knew that outwardly they would have to share me with other young people (our players); however, inwardly they had to think I was the biggest hypocrite ever. What I share with you now completely changed my life and the way I have coached the last 28 years.

One day when coming home, I walked through the front door and there stood my wife and two daughters. My heart immediately sank and I said, "What is wrong?" Well, my wife had name tags on my daughters. You know the ones that say *Hello, My Name is* _____. One tag said Hello, My Name is Tracey; the other said Hello, My Name is Ashley. My wife simply said to me that these two young ladies were so proud of me and what I was doing for young people, but they both needed a Dad, and so did our family.

Wow. My wife needed a husband, and my daughters needed a Dad. From then on, my coaching life was suddenly put into perspective and since then it has always included my wife, daughters, son-in-laws, and now three of the best grandchildren a person could ever have. Young coaches or even elder coaches, may we all keep things in perspective and in order: Faith, Family, and Football.

JAY MINTON

FOOTBALL'S LASTING LEGACY

The story I am going to share is about when I became the Head Coach at Northwest High School in Cincinnati, Ohio. I came across a 6'3", 215-pound sophomore that (little did I know) would become the closest thing to a son I would have. His name was Rasheen Jones, and the first thing that I can remember about him was his size and that, according to my eyeball test, he was quite a specimen and had the potential to be a big-time college football player. That is where the relationship started: Wanting to push a young man with all the potential to be the best version of himself. Over the next three years, I discovered that this young man's heart was also large. He had a wonderful smile and people loved him. Prior to high school, Rasheen would grow up with a mother that was an alcoholic and was in and out of homeless shelters numerous times. He had moved in with his aunt and uncle during the junior high years because it was a better situation for him.

Our car rides to and from practice, school, recruiting visits, etc., remain near and dear to my heart. One unique story about Rasheen was related to a poem he wrote his senior year. His English teacher just raved to me about it, and she had submitted it to a poetry contest that was being held in Cincinnati. Rasheen was chosen from among students in the Cincinnati area to read his poem at the Public Library in downtown Cincinnati. It was during that walk into the library in downtown Cincinnati that I found out that Rasheen and his friends used to walk to this library when they were little kids and access the internet because they did not have it at home. Now, years later, he walks into this same library to receive recognition for a poem that he had written. There was a time I almost obtained custody of Rasheen. But I did not need official government paperwork to treat this young man like he was the son I never had.

Rasheen ended his senior year with approximately 25 offers: West Virginia, Louisville, UK, to name a few. I can still remember Rick Minter telling me that he was an NFL kid, as he was the DC for Joker Phillips at UK at the time. He was versatile as an OLB/DE that could rush off the edge, or drop into coverage. He ended up committing to the University of Cincinnati and Tommy Tuberville. After efforts from numerous team members and his Northwest family, Rasheen did not end up qualifying and was forced to go the JUCO route. I vividly remember the day my wife and I dropped him off at the bus station for his chapter at Copiah Lincoln. While at Copiah Lincoln, he found out unintentionally that he was going to be "redshirted". Without understanding, he took this as a negative and was on a bus back to Cincinnati before I could speak with him. At that time, he didn't realize UC wanted three seasons to have him. After being home for a brief period, he headed out to a Div. III in Iowa. He spent a few years there and got to play the sport he loved.

He eventually made his way back to Cincinnati. I remember later taking a position at Hamilton High School and calling Rasheen to talk. I wanted to get him involved with our program. I knew he had a lot to offer, not only being a good player, but because of the size of his heart. Rasheen coached for me for a few years at Hamilton. He was a sponge for knowledge and scheme. The kids loved him. Rasheen now has four kids. He is a PHENOMENAL father. The father he never had. He coaches his son's pee wee team. I've been to observe a few times. It's awesome to watch a former player coaching his 6-year-old son in football.

No, this wasn't a "Blind Side" story of a kid coming from nothing to the NFL. This was a story about a young man coming from nothing, making himself into one of the best football players around, failing due to academics, standing back up and giving back to the youth through coaching the game of football. And now coaching his own son. Taking part in his son's life and the lives of his other kids. A father/son relationship that he did not get to experience with his own biological father. He is giving back. He is working and providing. He is a great dad and takes care of his family. The things that matter most. And mostly because of relationships and the game of football.

CHAD MURPHY
Winton Woods Football
2012 AP Div II State of Ohio COY
@coachchadmurphy

A TRIBUTE TO JOHN JOHNSON

Yesterday's news that John Johnson had passed away was devastating – devastating to me personally, but also devastating to anyone who has ever spent even a minute with John. What he meant to this program and to everyone who was touched by him cannot be described in words. I was already here at school when I heard the news yesterday morning, and all I could do was sit in my car and cry. I've been crying on and off ever since. I have coached at Randolph-Macon for 17 years, and I have been around some incredible young men, but I have never coached or been around anyone who was anything like John Johnson, or "John John", as he was affectionately known by all. He was too good to be true. If you had never met him and I told you about him, you would think I was describing someone you had read about in a book or maybe seen in a movie – but not a real-life character. He was that unique, and that awesome. No one that has ever come through here was better liked or more loved. And no one loved Randolph-Macon, Randolph-Macon football or his teammates more than John. One of my favorite passages in scripture is from Psalm 139, when King David describes the miracle of human conception and birth: "For you created my inmost being; you knit me together in my mother's womb. I praise you because I am fearfully and wonderfully made." As I have thought about John the last two days, I have reflected about how carefully God crafted him and knit him together, and what an amazing creation and gift he was. Fearfully and wonderfully made – no better words describe John. There has never been anyone like him, and there never will be. John's passing is tragic, but I am so grateful for the gift of his life and the time we all got to spend with him. As a coach you try not to have favorites, but that is impossible in this case. John brought light to a sometimes-dark world. He was, as my son Will said this morning when I asked him what he remembered most about John, "the most joyful and upbeat guy I have ever known."

John John came to Randolph-Macon from Nelson County High School in the fall of 2006. His teammate, JR Howard, was already here when we recruited John. John was all country. When I met him, I did not know what to make of him. I don't think any of us did. John was extremely quiet and soft-spoken – yes, that is true. He had never been away from home and was quite insecure and unsure about his new environment. When John showed up for football camp his freshman year, we had the first of many unique encounters. Anyone who knows John knows exactly what I am talking about. He had an uncanny way of sneaking up on you or showing up when you least expected him to. I was sitting in my office the morning after the players reported to camp, trying to get ahead on some work, when John silently slipped into my office. It was August, but it was still dark outside, and it was eerily quiet in the football offices when I looked at my watch and saw that it was 5 am. I was worried that he might already be homesick and want to leave, but he looked at me and said that he had just done a tour of the campus so that he would not be late to anything. In his own words, he said, "I took myself on a brief tour of the campus because I had such a hell of a time remembering where certain facilities were, such as Estes, Copley, Haley, and even my own dorm." He sat down in my office, and we talked for a while. I did not want to be rude, but I told John I had a few things to get done before practice. He did not mind, he said, and he sat there quietly while I worked, and then we walked to breakfast together. For several mornings he did the same thing. I reminded him that I did not want to be rude but that I had work to do, and he once again said that he wouldn't mind just sitting and hanging out. That  was the start of a wonderful and awesome relationship. When I gave John a spot on our roster, I did so because I thought this program might help change his life; instead, he changed mine.

I am fighting back tears as I write this. This guy was special. He was unbelievable. He was the best. His personality was bigger than life itself; his heart was even bigger. When you encountered John, you did not want to just shake his hand, you wanted to wrap your arms around him and hug him. He was just a lovable guy. If you are around someone long enough you will find something you do not like about them. You will find that everybody has a dark side. Not John. He did not have a bad bone in his body.

I have too many stories about John and not enough time to write them. Like I said, he would show up at the most unexpected times in the most unexpected of places. Years ago, my family was driving through campus early one Sunday morning on the way to church. It was the middle of summer and the campus was empty, when one of my boys said, "Hey dad, there's John John." It was July. No one was around. John had graduated years earlier. I thought he had seen someone else, but I looked in the rear view mirror, and yes, it was John, just walking the campus he loved. He loved this school and this football program. He graduated, but he never left. Randolph-Macon became his home. For years after he graduated, he would text me the week before the Hampden-Sydney game and ask if he could ride on the bus and stand on the sideline during the game. I know it meant a lot to him; it meant even more to me that he would want to do that. His love for this program and its players ran deep.

John had a servant heart like no one I have ever known. He was the gentlest of giants. Joyful, humble, and loyal. There has never been a more loyal guy than John Johnson. His words were not empty. When he said he would fight for you, he meant it. He once got so mad over a post written by someone who was critical of our program that he wrote me and said, "That comment reminded me of the old proverb from Abraham Lincoln: 'Tis better to remain silent and be thought a fool, than to open one's mouth and remove all doubt.' SHOW THIS JACKASS WHY HE COULDN'T HANG WITH THE BIG DOGS BY COMPETING AND BEATING ALL OF THE OPPOSITION!!!!!!! POUND THE ROCK!!!!!" John was loyal to the core. To John, loyalty was not just a word you put on a t-shirt or hung on a wall. He lived it every single day.

John never asked for anything in return. He gave and he gave, and he

gave. After he tore his ACL for the second time and had to retire from football, he volunteered to be our team manager. He was so passionate and committed to his role that I gave him the title of DFO (Director of Football Operations). He took this title and ran with it, even staying for a 5th year and serving this program. He said if he could have, he would have stayed here doing that forever. One of my favorite memories of John came during the Hampden-Sydney game in 2008, John's senior year. We had fallen behind 21-10 and lost our starting tailback to a knee injury going into the 4th quarter. We scored, missed the extra point, scored again, and converted on a 2-pt conversion to go up 24-21. As Hampden-Sydney drove down the field, our defense forced a fumble that Tristan Carr returned 65 yards for a touchdown to seemingly seal the win and an ODAC Championship. In the excitement of it all, however, John ran down the sidelines to celebrate and was flagged with a 15-yard unsportsmanlike penalty. The image is etched in my mind – John sprinting down the sideline beyond the coaches box, WAY beyond the coaches box, and then slipping and falling on his back when he tried to stop himself on the muddy sideline. I wanted to get mad, but I could not. It was John John, and as my son Owen said to me earlier today, "He was one of your favorite guys ever, like that you've ever met." It is true. He was, and always will be.

I will share a few more memories. On the morning of November 16, 2013, right before we played Hampden-Sydney for the ODAC Championship, I got a letter in my inbox from John. It was one of the best letters I have ever received from a former player, maybe the best. In it, he called himself "a very proud Pedro Arruza guy." It touched me then, but now those words pierce my heart. Losing that game was one of the hardest experiences of my professional career, but reading that letter again yesterday put a lot of things into perspective. That game is over and done, but the relationship I had with John trumps it all. When you are approaching 47, the wins mean a lot less, and you realize the stuff that you have chased all your life does not matter nearly as much as the relationships that you've built. I would not trade what I had with John for any win.

I will tell one more story that captures the essence of this kind, patient, and gentle soul. In July of 2013, I had come home from the beach a couple of days early to prepare for the season. I was scrambling. There was a ton to do and not enough time. I was the only one in the office when John showed up around 3:00 pm. He never called to tell me he was coming. He never did. He showed up in his work "uniform," name tag and all, and announced that he just wanted to see how I was doing. Like the day when he showed up at 5:00 am in 2006, I wanted to spend time with him – but I also had things that I had to get done. We talked for about an hour and then I told John that I really had to get some things done. He smiled and told me to go right ahead, that he would just sit there and hang with me while I finished my work. I don't know if he ever actually verbalized that, but he sat there with me until well after 10:00 pm, when I finally went home. Neither of us said much. We did not have to. It was a great night.

John was a patient, joyful, loving, and loyal spirit. He had a still and gentle presence that is hard to describe. John found a way to lift your spirits. He did this even when he wasn't trying to. He was one of the most thoughtful and intelligent human beings that I have ever been around. He was simple and perceptive in a way that few are. John did not suffer fools. He knew if you were a phony, and he had no tolerance for that. John was exuberant, spirited, and even crazy at times, but if you watched him carefully, he would often sit back and survey the scene. He was very observant and there was a depth to him that few people realize. John was passionate about the things he loved. He loved wrestling. The picture in the beginning of this story is from December of 2015, when a few of John's old teammates and I went to watch him wrestle. He loved wrestling, and he pursued his passion with an enthusiasm unknown to mankind.

Lastly, John was one of the funniest guys that I have ever known. His texts made me laugh out loud. I went back and looked at some of the texts we exchanged over the years. One minute I was laughing and the next I was crying again. He was truly hilarious. I asked a few years ago if he liked his new roommate. He responded by saying, "Yep. A hell of a lot better than living with someone with the build of Bigfoot and the mindset of Baby Huey." John could be funny as heck. He was clever and witty and had a way with words.

My last text exchange with him was over Christmas. I do not know why I texted him. I told him I was just thinking about him. He wanted to know if he could come to the games in the spring as long as he socially distanced. He loved coming to football games. He assured me we would continue to dominate the ODAC. He wanted to know how Owen was doing at Randolph-Macon. He told me he loved me. John's capacity to love was unlike any other.

John, may you rest in peace. You were, and are, a gift to this world, but heaven is a better place today because you are there. I can picture you up there now, making everybody laugh, wrestling and never getting tired or sore, looking down on us and smiling because you know that soon we will meet again. Rest easy, buddy. I love you and so does everyone who has ever crossed paths with you. You are going to be missed ... but not forgotten.

COACH ARRUZA

SPORTS ILLUSTRATED

In 1990 I was a young coach at Franklin High School. We had a QB named Shawn Lamb that threw for over 300 yards in a game, which was unheard of at that time.

The next week a parent brought me a copy of *Sports Illustrated* that had a little blurb about a QB from Franklin, Ohio, throwing for over 300 yards in a game and it mentioned that the coach must know the passing game well.

A couple days later I was in my upstairs bathroom shaving and the phone rang. My wife answered and then yelled, "John ... Sports Illustrated wants to talk to you!" I about cut my chin off, I ran down the steps so fast. I was so excited knowing *Sports Illustrated* was going to do an article on me.

I grabbed the phone and said excitedly, "This is Coach John Aregood!"

A female voice on the phone said, "Mr. Aregood, for twelve dollars and ninety-five cents we will send you the next three issues of Sports Illustrated!"

Of course, I was embarrassed and deflated.

COACH JOHN AREGOOD

HIT-ITS

In 2003, Steve Woods asked me to coach his freshman football team. He knew the players and their parents were trouble, and he wanted a veteran coach that could handle them. They were a tough bunch of kids and parents to work with.

On the bus ride home from our first game the players were out of control so I told them, "Tomorrow at practice we will do 200 hit-its."

The next day before practice my assistant coach told me that the kids were going to walk off and quit when I tell them to do hit-its and that the parents are all lined up in cars by the practice field and are going to attack me as a group when the kids walk off.

I thought for a minute and told my assistant to bring out a camcorder. He asked if we had any tapes and I told him we wouldn't need one.

After warming up the team I said, "I heard you are all walking off and quitting when I tell you to do hit-its. I also see your parents in their cars watching to see what happens. If you want to do that you are welcome to. Just strip down to your underwear now, leave our equipment here on the field and walk to school in the only thing you have (your underwear). And by the way, Coach Rippl is going to video tape this and send it to Funniest Home Videos". The players looked at each other for a minute and started doing their hit-its.

COACH JOHN AREGOOD

GOAL SETTING

I am a firm believer in setting goals: short, medium, and long-term future goals. As a football coach I would meet with each of our players twice a year, and they were expected to talk about their individual goals.

At the conclusion of their eligibility and during their "exit interview" the question was always asked: "Ten years from now, where will you be living and what will be your occupation"? We had one quarterback who struggled to get quality playing time during his college career. When we sat down and conducted his exit interview, he said to me, "I don't know what I will be doing in 10 years, but by the time I am 40 years old I will be the head football coach for the University of Michigan!" I thought to myself, this young man has always demonstrated great drive, but he could not get much playing time at a non-scholarship program and he believes he is going to be the head football coach at the University of Michigan! Seriously?

Well, he continued to set and achieve short-term goals with a long-term plan! At the age of 39, after assistant coaching positions in college and the NFL, he became the head coach for the Oakland Raiders. He turned down numerous other head coaching jobs and won a Super Bowl as the Tampa Bay Buccaneers' head coach. That back-up QB was Jon Gruden.

Bottom line is: keep your head down, believe in yourself and keep chopping wood and working every day. You can achieve your ultimate goals.

MIKE KELLY
Former Head Coach
University of Dayton Flyers

GRUDEN PAYS FORWARD

You know, coaching has brought so many joys into my life. I'm talking everything: from the amazing players I've coached, to coaches I've coached with, to the support staff and administrators you see every day. The list can go on and on. You always remember the big-time wins, the heart-breaking losses, the players on opposing teams that you coached against that stuck with you. It's why the annual coaches' convention every year is so great because you get to tell these stories and live those memories again with the guys you experienced them with, and hear other stories from other coaches that just make you smile and laugh. All of this makes every 5am workout group or 2am game plan session so worth it. No one quite understands the coaching life unless they have been a coach themselves.

But for me, one of my favorite coaching memories that has stuck with me for years, and will stick with me my entire life, came at the NFL Combine in 2018. College coaches are allowed to attend the combine, watch the workouts, and hang out in Indianapolis for as long as they wish. It's an amazing thing for the NFL to allow college coaches to do this. But this particular memory was from a Saturday night at the Hyatt hotel right across the street from the convention center. My buddy Chris and I were hanging out in the hotel bar late, after coming from dinner at Harry and Izzy's. Several NFL coaches were also just hanging out and just having a good time.

Well, Jon Gruden and his brother Jay were hanging out in the hotel bar and having a great time. Jon had just come back into the NFL as head coach of the then Oakland Raiders.

Now I had met Jon back in 2015 when I was on staff at the University of Dayton. Trust me, I knew he did not remember me from the bartender, but I had also just come from hanging out earlier in the day with Darrell Hazell. Darrell at the time was the wide receivers coach for the Minnesota Vikings. Darrell and Jon know each other well from when they attended Muskingum University as college freshman.

Well, I was coaching at Muskingum at the time, so I decided to walk over to Jon Gruden and say hello to him. I will never forget this if I live. I walked over, introduced myself, told him where I was coaching and where I had met him previously.

When I said the word Muskingum, Jon, in his classic Gruden voice, said, "The Muskies" and when I said Dayton, he said "The Flyers." He of course knows Darrell well and said awesome things about him, and then pounded on my chest with the classic Gruden fist and told me to keep doing great things.

The reason this sticks with me is, well, it is Jon Gruden for one. Anyone that coaches football in some way considers Gruden to be a great coach. But what sticks with me more is how awesome he was to me. He did not know me, could've easily brushed me off but took less than five minutes to say hey and encourage me for what I was doing. Really shows exactly who he is as a person. Every coach has a huge list of great memories and stories in this awesome profession of ours, and I am glad I could share one of my favorite memories.

MIKE KELLY

ANSWERING THE PHONE MIGHT CHANGE A LIFE!

On December 22, 1995, I received a phone call from Phillip Fulmer: he wanted to speak to our head coach, Carlton Flatt, regarding recruiting. I told Coach Fulmer that Coach Flatt was not on campus. Fulmer then asked to speak with either Coach Ray Dalton or Coach Jimmy Gentry. Coach Fulmer and other UT assistant coaches were very familiar with both assistant coaches; Dalton played at UT from 1959-1963 and Coach Gentry was a fixture in our community. I let Coach Fulmer know that exams were over, and all our coaches were "gone" for Christmas break. (I only caught the phone call because I was in the football office to make a few copies of game film.)

Coach Fulmer commenced to tell me his staff was putting the finishing touches on recruiting but would like to add one or two in-state players to this recruiting class. He wanted to know the best player we played against that year, who he should be considering, etc. I point blank told him that the best unsigned player that I knew of was on our roster, and I gave him the name Mikki Allen. Mikki had recently played a tremendous State Semi-final game against Clarksville Northeast.

I told Coach Fulmer that I was convinced that Mikki Allen could play at a high level after seeing his performance against Clarksville Northeast, as I saw him tackle Stephens in the open field several times. Fulmer asked me if I could make a copy of the State Semi-final game, to which I replied, "Sure." He asked me to FedEx Overnight the tape to a hotel in South Carolina, where he was on the road recruiting. The week following Christmas, Mikki informed me of the good news: he had received a scholarship offer from the University of Tennessee. The rest is history. Mikki played four years at UT, being a key role player and contributing to the National Championship win in 1998. After a brief stint in the NFL, Mikki parlayed his contacts and network with teammates to build a successful business, which he eventually sold.

Allen was then hired by the University within the Athletic Department to assist with alumni and player relations, and fundraising. Dr. Mikki Allen was recently hired as the new Athletic Director at Tennessee State University.

ANONYMOUS

IT WAS WORTH ALL THE PAIN

During one of my first seasons of coaching, I had the great challenge of taking over a veteran receiving crew. One of the returners, Ricky, was a national statistical leader in receiving yards and as a punt returner. He was up for some all-American pre-season honors. He was like many great players: very confident in his ability, and cocky, but he was really focused on his stats and his success first. Not a great ingredient for team success, but he worked hard and made plays, so you had to accept some of the rough edges. As a coach, you want all areas to be complete. So, my task was to develop this playmaker to continue to make plays *and* become a selfless leader. Make the entire receiving better. Week one, Ricky has his customized uniform on. Every wrist band, forearm, calf bands, wrist tape, etc. He was pushing the "look at me" approach. We would need to address that so it would not become a problem, as it relates to a uniform consistency, not an individual look.

We were playing a longtime rival for game one, and we jumped out to a lead and Ricky was making plays as a returner and receiver. He played his best with the lights on – he loved to compete. As this game does to you so often, Ricky and our team got a reality check at the end of the 2nd quarter. Ricky had caught a drag route and was making guys miss when he stuck his foot in the ground and had a defender collision him from the side. His knee buckled and he went down in agony. It looked awkward and unfortunately he tore the knee up bad.

ACL and MCL surgery was needed the next week. Ricky's life changed dramatically and it was tough. He had gone from the play-making stallion to not being able to get off the couch. It was a slap to his confidence and mentally he was a mess. Having been through a knee injury myself, I tried to encourage him to rehab and that he could come back. He was more worried about the loss of his status, possibility of All League, All-American awards, career records, etc. It bothered me but I let him vent, hoping that he would get through this mourning period. He did not; about 3 weeks post-surgery, he was a slug, hardly moving off the couch, and his academics where slipping. He was a business major; he once said he was going to be the next Wolf of Wall Street. I decided to bring in my secret weapon, Joe Sirva.

Joe was a legendary local athlete in multiple sports before being drafted into the Army. He was shipped off to Vietnam as an infantry soldier. He came back in a wheelchair missing both legs from the thigh down. He had stepped on a land mine. But he never missed a beat and was the most positive man I had ever met. He would always say, I may not be able to dance at my daughter's wedding, but I'll be there, and that's better than the 57 guys who were KIA the day I lost my legs.

He rolled up to Ricky's door, turned to me, and said, "I'll take it from here." Ricky answered the door, shocked. Joe told Ricky to back up, he could hop his chair up a step: he was a bad ass. About 45 minutes later he hops off the doorstep and says, "Let's roll." I looked back and Ricky looked pale. En route home, I asked, how did it go? Joe paused and said, "Damn, that kid is selfish!" He said he listened to Ricky, then read him the battle call. Told him to stop feeling sorry for his skinny ass. You got both legs. Work hard to fix the knee. If you want to play again, earn it. Ricky and Joe became friends. Ricky was growing through this adversity.

Fast forward to the next spring, and Ricky was looking good. He was ahead of schedule for August return. But he was also helping the young guys and becoming a selfless leader. I was amazed at who he was becoming as a young man.

Then reality hit *again*. He was getting that swagger back and was at a party, jumped off a few steps, and tore the ACL in the *other* knee. We all felt terrible for him. But he did not — he instead attacked everything: rehab, studies, leadership.

He really was becoming an All-American! Because of the second injury, he was going to mis the entire season. He was a coach's dream. He helped with all aspects of our young guys. He verbalized, coached, encouraged, and dissected plays and fundamentals. I told him how proud I was of him one day, and he says thanks, coach. I get what a selfless teammate is. It's not about me, it's about we/us. He also said he was changing majors and would go into physical rehab, maybe even work with amputee victims. Wow!

He was not the same player the next year, but he was a leader in every way. As the season progressed, his time was limited. He was not able to return kicks or punts, so he had gone from being "the guy" to a possession receiver at best. We were battling for a league championship and along the way Ricky made three big catches. One for a 1st down conversion, another on a 2 pt play, and another to help run time off and win field position. After one of his 3 catches for the entire year, he came over to the bench and tears were running down his cheeks. I said, "Ricky what's wrong?" He said, "Coach, it was all worth it – all the pain and rehab, I was humbled, and I am better for it!"

I was amazed and humbled by this scene and who Ricky had become. As I turned around, I saw Joe in his wheelchair at the top of the stands, and I gave him a thumbs up. He smiled and saluted back!

MTE

NEXT MAN UP!

I personally believe one of the greatest joys in coaching is watching a "non-starter" shine in a big-time moment, because you as the coach never coached that player any differently and that player prepared like the starter. One moment that comes to mind for me came in the 2014 season, when I was coaching at the University of Dayton. We traveled to Davidson, North Carolina, and, man, was this one of those games you will never forget. A 54-48, 5 overtime game. Yes, I wrote that correctly…5 overtimes. An absolute back-and-forth game that really got going in the fourth quarter and obviously the overtime segments.

I was coaching in the secondary, and going into the game we were already down one of our starting corners. So, we are battling back and forth, defensive battle for most of the game. Well, the third quarter comes around and my number two corner gets hurt making a great play breaking up and pass. Trainer comes to me after evaluating the young man and tells me he is done for the game. So now I have a true freshman who started this game because of the injury to my number one corner, and now I bring in my number four corner to finish the game right when things get hot! Now for all you coaches out there, everyone knows that you attack "fresh meat," right? Well, this case was not any different. Davidson had a very talented and athletic QB and he went right at my brand new, fresh-off-the-sideline corner. Now I will say, this young man played very well. The moment never got too big and his emotions never got too high or too low. He gave up some deep passes and I believe maybe even a touchdown or two, but again, you would not have been able to tell by the way he carried himself.

As we were going back and forth in the overtime segments, all the touchdowns were coming on the ground. We had an All-American RB who just could not be stopped, and Davidson was doing a great job using the QB as a runner and catching us defensively in odd numbers. Well, we roll into the fifth overtime, and I mean, my heart is pounding. Heavyweight match-up, who will break first, all those feelings. Our offense goes right down and scores quickly. Now it is the fifth overtime so no PATs at this point. Everything is going for two. Well, we do not convert. So, it's 54-48 and now Davidson is on offense. We told ourselves as a staff that this QB will need to beat us with his arm, not his feet. So we are going to bring some pressure and keep him in the pocket and make him throw. I want to say it was 2nd down. QB drops back and tries to throw a hitch route to his field wide receiver. Well, my man Tommy Fanning, who was my number four corner, and who I nicknamed "The Technician," comes bursting out of his break and makes a great interception on the ball. GAME OVER! I went absolutely nuts like the rest of our sideline did, and our fans who made the trip down to North Carolina! Tommy is an amazing young man, and he treated every single practice like a true professional; he was ready for that moment. Fifth overtime, on the road, hostile environment, and he is the one who seals the deal for the Flyers! It was amazing!

I know all of you coaches out there have a story that you can relate to like this one, but these are the moments that you coach for. Your "starters" should be making plays. That is why they are the starters. But in my opinion, when a player comes off the bench and makes a big-time play under the big spotlight because that player does it all right every single day: *that* is what should put a smile on your face. Tommy Fanning was that type of player for me at Dayton.

COACH CODY CRUZEN

EXPAND YOUR HUDDLE THROUGH ATHLETICS

My name is Chip Otten, and I am 61 years old. Today I am teaching and coaching at Coldwater High School in Ohio. I grew up in Kettering, Ohio, a suburb of Dayton. From as early as I can remember, maybe 5 years old, I was always playing multiple sports in the neighborhood and going to football practices and sporting events with my father ("Coach Barney") at Dayton Carroll HS, Bellbrook HS, and Stebbins HS.

My first experiences with organized football and baseball were at a little park named Ireland Field, across from the Kettering YMCA. What a great experience it was, playing with friends and other kids my age, without all the travel ball and AAU stuff of today. Had some great friends and talented athletes from the area that I got to know and compete with and against! Brady Hoke, Jim Schumann, John Paxon, Ed Schmidt, Jim Nowicki, to name just a few, that all ended up playing college football, basketball, or baseball.

At the time I didn't realize my relationship huddle was beginning and expanding as each year went by. During the mid-1970s, my dad was coaching with the legendary Hank Snyder (father of long-time Dayton area Coach Mike) and Hall of Famer Jim Place, and they were coaching good friend Bob Thompson, who I would eventually coach with at Middletown HS.

So as I got into high school, I moved with my family to Coldwater, where my Dad took over the head football job and the huddle got expanded even more with new friends, classmates and teammates.

To make a long story a little shorter, my athletic and coaching career took me to Bowling Green, where I played football and was GA coach for a year after graduation. Interesting side note: I was reunited at BG, playing with longtime friend Jim Schumann and playing against the Hoke brothers, who were at Ball State. From there I was a GA at Ball State for one year, and then spent two years at Indiana University working under Bill Mallory, who was a great mentor for me as a young coach.

As I moved on into the late 80s, I entered the high school coaching world working for Coach Place. As you can imagine, I had some great

THE ARENA — STAND TALL

experiences and met so many great people over those years as my huddle kept expanding. As Coach Place moved on, I coached at Middletown for 8 more years, then one year at Valley View under Hall of Famer Jay Niswonger and his great staff.

The final chapter has me back in Coldwater for the past 21 years (thanks to Tim Hoyng for reaching out to get me back to Coldwater), both as an assistant under Hall of Famer John Reed and now in my 11th year as head coach. In these Coldwater years I have gotten to experience coaching my three sons, coaching with 15 to 20 great coaches, and have been a part of 7 state championships to share with parents, friends, players, and the Coldwater community. Go Cavs!

The point of my story is that I have met and built so many positive relationships through sports and teaching. I feel like I have never really worked a day in my life. I get to hang out with kids and coaches and my family every day of my life!

Build and expand your huddle year after year!

Thanks to Mark for including me and asking me to write a little story. A side note is that Mark and my Dad coached together at Carroll in his later years. Also, special thanks to my wife, Diane, for being a great coach's wife, and my children, Samantha, Brady, Troy, and Drew, for being great kids who have become mature, caring, productive, fun, and independent young adults.

ANONYMOUS

All the Years a Tough Price to Play

Total Commitment Day by Day

Learning and Teaching the Right Approach

No Title Greater than to be Called Coach

COACH SHEEHAN

I CAN CATCH IT, COACH!

I'll never forget those words and how it changed my view and approach to coaching. It was my third year of coaching, and we had a chance to be pretty competitive. I felt if we stayed healthy, we could challenge for the mountain Valley championship in 1995. The area we really needed to improve was the kicking game. We had a freshman kicker with no experience and a new center, and really were struggling, on top of that, holding on PAT and field goals.

We had open tryouts at camp, and that's when Eddie Casper, a manager, said "I can catch it, Coach." We kept dropping the snaps that most of the time were all over the place. Eddie had been born with a deformed foot and struggled to walk, let alone run. He had been a manager in camp and he had a great attitude.

Coach Smith convinced me that he would give him some pointers and we ought to look at him. Smitty said that he could focus on just catching snaps and help the whole unit. I begrudgingly agreed. I would regret my attitude later and hopefully learned from it. Eddie and the other candidates had 10 snaps to catch to see who would be the one we would work with the most moving ahead. The first 3 where pretty inconsistent at best. The number to top was 5 catches out of 10.

Well Eddie knelt down and with great confidence snagged 8 out of 10 like a real holder. The team rallied around Eddie, and he made every one better. He worked tirelessly at it. He kept improving and made the snapper and kickers better as well, because he wanted to get extra work in all the time. It was paying off: we became a team with a consistent kicking game because of his attitude and relentless work ethic.

The one area of concern was how would he handle a bad snap. Well he worked at that too. He practiced catching a high snap or low, getting the ball in both hands, and pushing himself up with the ball and rolling to the right to throw a fairly wobbly but effective pass. The team could see how uncomfortable it was to put pressure on his thin, deformed legs.

I asked our captain what he thought about Eddie ,and he point blank said, we are a better, tougher team because of Eddie. He's our MVP. Well we had some great players and we were winning games, and we ended up tied with the Gold Mountain Lions. We ended up winning the game 27-24 on a late field goal with Eddie getting a low snap down flawlessly. We were champions led by some great leaders and players and by an inspiring young man. Eddie Casper inspired us and taught me and the team to focus on what you can do and get better at it, not to focus on what you can't control, like two bad legs. Eddie Casper, our holder, received, and rightfully so, the award of the Most Inspiring Player of the Year.

Eddie taught me to look at each young man's upside — what he can do to help the team be its best, not the limitations he may have.

Thanks, Eddie, for speaking up and saying "I can catch it, Coach!" You made a huge difference and inspired the Championship Team in 1995 and opened our eyes, minds, and hearts to what a person with a disability can achieve.

MTE

I STILL HAVE FIVE

Growing up in rural Minnesota, the Bradley family loved to compete in everything. Be it hockey, basketball, football, frisbee golf in the corn fields, or Yahtzee at game night very Saturday night on their farm just east of St. Peter, Minnesota. Three boys and three girls were the pride and joy of Jim and Regina Weaver.

Jim was a hands-on father and the leader of this third-generation farm family as it related to hard work and an attitude of competing to be the best. He always barked to all his boys and girls: attack your competitor with passion and energy. Wear 'em down — outwork them!

Hard work was the credo of the Weaver clan. 500+ acres of farmland, and pigs and dairy cows, kept the entire family working every day. All the boys helped in the fields and the girls helped with the livestock. Regina homeschooled the kids until 8th grade. All the kids excelled in sports. Jim loved to work with all the kids each evening. The middle son, Jack, was the best athlete of all the kids. As a freshman he was the starting QB on the varsity team and starting pitcher, winning 10 games.

Every chance Jim had to spare some minutes away from the never-ending chores, he was throwing with Jack and his brothers. He had not played sports in high school because he always was working on the farm. His father told him he did not have time. Jim saw it differently; he wanted his children competing in any sport they wanted, and he demanded they do it with passion. His go-to sayings were many: "Attack that ball." "Outwork them." "Out-hustle 'em." When he threw baseball or football, it was always: "Get 10 fingers on it!" "Keep your eyes on it!"

The high school coaches told Jim that Jack would be a big-time recruit with continued hard work and improvement. Jim and Regina decided they would hire a full-time employee to help around the farm the next summer to allow Jack and all the kids to pursue sports and the extra work it took in the summer. That last summer, Jim pushed the kids hard. Each day up at 5 am, doing daily chores until noon. After lunch the never-ending chores kept all busy until 4 or 5.

Just before football season was to start for Jack, everything changed.

Jim constantly barked at all the kids to be safe, respect the machines, farming is hard work... and that farming won't kill you but the machines will. It was a Saturday morning in July. The heat was stifling, but a long-sleeved shirt had to be worn to protect your arms from scratches. Jack's older brother, Sam, was working on a grain auger when it happened. The auger was warming up when Sam tried to clean the edge of it with a broom. It caught him by the arm and pulled him into the machine and he died instantly. Jack heard the scream and ran into the barn. He was horrified and ran to help Sam; he reached into the machine to pull Sam out but it was too late, he couldn't budge him. The despair he was feeling was only eclipsed by the sharp pain he felt in his left arm. The last thing he remembered was the terrible pain. He woke up in the hospital a few days later, with his mom and dad in the room. He looked at his left arm and again he was horrified. He knew right then that a part of his arm was gone. He was wrapped up like a mummy, but he knew it. He also saw a look in his parents' eyes he had never seen before.

He was in the hospital for two weeks and everything seemed like a blur. There was the funeral and the never-ending grief he and his family felt. His arm had been torn off just above the elbow. He was starting rehab and felt his sports career was over. His father was depressed and felt responsible. Everything that seemed great days before had changed drastically.

It took months to start feeling somewhat normal. But his father just would not snap out of it. Jack decided he would change that. His rehab had picked up and his physical therapist motivated him like his father used to. He started to be able to catch a ball with his right arm and his stump. He was driven to show his Dad he could still play. He thought it might get him out of his funk.

He went into the barn one morning with a football and his baseball glove. His Dad was shocked and asked him what he wanted. Jack said, "We got to get back to work – we gotta start outworking them – wear 'em down!" His father started crying and he said, it's not the same. Jack said, "I know, but we are the Weavers. I am tougher than this. I am playing again, Dad." He continued: "Dad. Listen. I still got five fingers. I'll attack every ball with those. We gotta keep trying to compete – Sam would want us to, you know that!"

His Dad grabbed him and hugged him, and they cried together, and his father said he was right.

Well that's just what Jack did his senior year: he started as the QB and found a way to be second team All-League. He really excelled in baseball. He studied Jim Abbott and the fact that his throwing arm was intact and he could really throw. He had a glove fitted for his left hand with an attachment for his stump, and he got pretty good at stopping a ball when needed. He led his team to the district finals and has a 9-3 record. His family went on competing; his father got back to leading and working hard for his family. Jack kept astounding so many with his perseverance. He would go on to get his veterinarian license from the University of Minnesota.

It's not what happens to you, it's how you handle it!

MTE

FT. CAMPBELL — ARMY STRONG

During pre-season camp, I had two brothers on my team, a junior and senior. Their father, who was on a military mission, lost his eyesight when a roadside bomb exploded in his eyes. The boys left Kentucky on a Tuesday and demanded to return for practice on Thursday so they could play in the pre-season game. The team took that unfortunate situation as their motivation for the year. The team began 0-2, giving up 100 pts in the first two games. The team met after the second game with the coaches, we all got on the same page, and decided to stop focusing on a title and focus on ourselves. There was no more "For the Ring" and instead it became "Falcons." The team went on to win the next 13 games and the first state title since 1979. The boys' father was able to be present at the state championship game.

In summer of 2008, another player's father, this time of one of our seniors, was killed while testing a helicopter. It was devastating to say the least. Once again, the coaches rallied the players around this young man and gave him and his family all the love and support they needed. The battle cry for the season was "No Regrets." This young man was a very good player. In the state semi-final game, while down on the scoreboard, our defensive coordinator pulled him to the sideline and challenged him, referencing his father, who was watching him play from above. The young man went on to make the next 8 tackles, 3 of them for a loss. This singlehandedly was the greatest performance by a player in my 18 years of coaching. The team won the game, finished 14-1, and were back to back state champions.

In pre-season camp 2009, the team was having the second practice of the day. It was raining and 72 degrees: pleasant for a player to practice. As we were ending practice and came together as a team, one of the young men lost consciousness. We cleared the team from the field and called 911 and his mother. He came to and then fell unconscious again. He was rushed to the hospital, where he was put on life support. He died the next day. He was going into his junior season. Needless to say, this was shocking to the team. The coaches, team, and community rallied around his parents and kept them close. We used "Tim" as our motivation for the season. In the state title game, we trailed for the first time all season. Our head coach called time-out and brought the players together. He carried a 10x12 framed picture of Tim on the bus and kept it on the sideline. He held that picture up and said "We will win this for Tim and his memory." We went on to win the third state title in a row.

Needless to say, these were all tragedies a team should never have to go through. What separates these stories from others is the way the coaching staff mentored, loved, and coached these young men through the tragedies to bring about triumph. I've been a part of many staffs, but never have I been able to affect the lives of a team like I was able to in those three years.

By the way, in the winter of 2010, we lost one of our assistant coaches to an asthma attack. The rally cry for the 2011 season was "Coach T'. Although a state title was not achieved, it was not due to lack of purpose or motivation.

Thank you,
MIKE MARCIANO

MELISSA

Our family was the typical American sports family. Mom and Dad played sports in grade school and high school, and then played co-ed sports together after marriage. We had a daughter and a son and as soon as they could walk, they both learned to play sports. Both were very good in multiple sports in high school, and then in college our daughter played rugby, and our son, football. Needless to say, it was always very competitive around our house.

On the day of our 27th anniversary, our daughter Melissa came home with the worst news possible. She had been diagnosed with breast cancer.

She battled this new opponent with great courage and strength. She took chemo during lunch breaks… continued to play rugby, got married, lost her hair on several occasions, walked 60 miles in the three-day Susan G. Komen Walk in Atlanta, and never, ever gave up. She was living her life to the fullest on the outside, while fighting a painful battle on the inside, never complaining and never feeling sorry for herself.

She fought cancer for over five years. Two months before she passed away, she was admitted to the hospital. During her stay, the ONLY thing she complained about was the hospital gowns. She talked about designing a hospital gown that was not as revealing. Then she asked her dad to call our friend, the Athletic Department secretary, requesting a couple of Fairmont t-shirts (to wear in place of the hospital gowns!). The Athletic Department's response was unbelievable. In less than two hours, ten t-shirts and a basketball hoodie were delivered to the hospital by our friend, the AD Secretary! Two days later, t-shirts from every other sport at Fairmont were delivered to Melissa's room. The coaches' response to our daughter's small request was mind-boggling. She wore those shirts for the next three weeks and had one on the morning of Jan 3, 2009, when she took her last breath.

About nine months after her death, those same shirts were made into a quilt and raffled off at a fundraiser, raising $1,700 towards her scholarship fund! Her mother-in-law made the quilt, and one of Melissa's best friends won the quilt.

Melissa's family will never forget the acts of kindness from those coaches. To date, five $1,000 scholarships have been awarded to Fairmont students in Melissa's name. The scholarships will be awarded for many years to come, thanks to the generosity of the Fairmont community, her friends, family, and all of the Fairmont coaches.

DON FORTENER

A GAMER

If you are looking for stories, this one may be of interest. In 1986, I was coaching at Detroit Country Day, and we won the state Class C championship. Muskegon Catholic Central scored and went ahead with 2 minutes in the game. My QB came to me on the sideline and said, "We will win this game. We have all our timeouts left."

We went 80 yards in that 2 minutes and with 16 seconds and counting, Charles Johnson, our QB, audibled to a fade pass into the end zone and we scored the winning TD with no time on the clock. I know there are many games that end in such fashion. What makes this a unique story is what follows. "CJ" was a talented athlete and leader; however, his size, 5'11" and 175 lbs, was not what many colleges were looking for. I knew Colorado's coach, Bill McCartney, well from his days in Detroit. I told him about CJ and that I knew he would be a winner for them if given the chance. Bill said if he would walk on and do well in the spring, he would offer him a scholarship.

CJ did well and did get the scholarship. He was the backup QB most of his years. In 1991, Colorado played Notre Dame in the Orange Bowl. The starting QB got hurt and CJ came in to start the second half. He brought Colorado back to get the win, just like he did in high school. CJ was named MVP for that game. Look up "1991 Orange Bowl" on Google and you can get more of the facts. CJ presently is assistant Athletic Director at Colorado. A real winner.

JOE D'ANGELO

THE LASTING IMPACT OF A GRACIOUS MENTOR

In 1973 I had the honor of being named the Head Football Coach at the new Grayson County High School in Leitchfield, Kentucky, and the tremendous opportunity of starting a football program in a county that did not have a football program. Surprisingly, I was only 23 years old, just out of college, with no coaching experience. (My first year, the new county high school was not completed, so we organized 9th grade teams at each of the three small community high schools in the county that were being consolidated, and those teams played 9 game schedules that season, so 1974 was the first season of GCHS football.)

As we prepared for the 1974 season, my Assistant Principal, Bill Given, a friend of Western Kentucky Hilltopper head football coach Jimmy Feix, called him. Coach Feix agreed to help me ("a little") and he became the coaching mentor I never had.

At first, Coach Feix came to our high school, about 60 miles from WKU, and met with me a couple of times and helped me set up a head coach's Program Master Plan (yearly schedule), practice plans, and daily, weekly, and season schedules. He always emphasized that I was to teach the fundamentals of blocking and tackling.

A great piece of advice Coach Feix gave me was to always surround myself with great people as my coaches. The first two assistants I got to hire at Grayson County High were Don Rawlings, and WKU grad and Grayson County native Bill Embry. Between those two men they eventually served as Head Football Coach of GCHS about 25 years. I am extremely proud to have been associated with such fine men and coaches while at Grayson County Kentucky.

After those initial meetings, Coach Feix always found time throughout the year to meet with me in his office. The discussions were about making a difference in the lives of the young men we coach, and how that was a bigger part of our responsibility than the game of football itself. Having fun with our players was also important to Coach Feix. He told me to be sure to *enjoy* being a football coach.

During the season, Coach Feix would always have tickets for me and my wife waiting at the gate on game day. We'd always enjoy the game, but that too was such a learning experience (game management, sideline management, clock management, Coach Feix's interaction with players, pre-game organization, etc). I learned so much about coaching just by observing Coach Feix, then having an opportunity to discuss some of it with him by phone.

One of the greatest lessons I learned from Coach Feix, that I still consciously use today, was to make sure that every boy in your program know that "he is important."

ANONYMOUS

WHAT FOOTBALL IS ALL ABOUT

In a record-setting year and a number of players reaching milestones, Senior Tim Adkins recorded his one and only career varsity tackle for the 2013 Wheelersburg Pirate Football Team. Tim's impact on the program, and more importantly, the program's impact on him, was one that cannot be statistically measured. To understand the whole scope of this player's journey, one must begin with his freshman year at Wheelersburg HS.

Tim was a freshman in my physical science class. He dressed in all black, ragged, torn clothing, and his long hair didn't allow anyone to really see his face. Tim struck me as one who didn't care much for the structure of school and his attendance and grades reflected just that. Tim's face was often buried in a book and yet he quickly showed signs of being very intelligent. Tim was not challenged at the level he needed to be in any of the classes he had his freshman year, and with his absences above 100 days, he ended up failing that year.

Entering his sophomore year, Tim was repeating all of the same material, scoring As on tests, but not caring to complete classwork, and he would receive a C for the year. During his sophomore year Tim came out for winter weights with the football team. Tim's coordination and athletic ability were minimal, but one could tell that he had the desire to be better. During the first week we lifted, we were running on the parking lot and Tim tripped and scraped his whole back up; it was bleeding through his torn shirt. Tim only lasted a few more weeks, then as the weather broke in the spring, he drifted away like many others tend to.

The next year Tim improved himself in the classroom and again came out for weights. This time he was a little more driven. His attendance was a little better and one could tell he was starting to feel both challenged, and a sense of belonging. That spring I had the 2013 potential players fill out some information for me so I could order some items needed for the fall. I always have the players answer one question in a well-written complete sentence: What are your goals for the 2013 football season? Tim's answer was as follows: "To improve myself on an athletic and disciplinary level. I believe the Wheelersburg Football Program puts me in an environment that teaches me goodwill, discipline, and respect. I hope to improve myself in that environment, not as a player or an athlete but as a person." Well I was impressed to say the least; I hoped that every member of the team was thinking this same idea, but to have one write it down and turn it in --- well I don't get many of those.

While I was impressed, I knew it was a far stretch to get Tim Adkins to commit to anything as tough as summer weights, two-a-day practices, and the length of an entire season. Tim had no means of travel; he had no clothes to really wear each day. So I asked him where he lived and paired him with one of our senior captains, Cam, who lived close to Tim's house, and asked if he would help ensure that Tim had a ride to practice. Cam agreed and told Tim he had better be there and be ready. Tim showed up the first day, and every day after, until one day Cam was late and had to run. Cam returned to Tim's house and demanded a reason why, and communicated that it had better not happen again or there would be no more rides to practice. Tim promised it wouldn't and held to that promise, and the two were the first at nearly every practice.

During one trip home from practice, Tim asked Cam if he would care to stop for something to eat. Cam responded, "Sure? Why? Are you hungry?" Tim then acknowledged that he had not had any food in two days because there was nothing to eat in their house. This struck Cam because he had never gone without, and for one of his teammates to not have food during summer practice really awakened him to differences in the world. Tim was never hungry again after that day.

But it was a second admittance by Tim that truly caused change in his life. Tim was dragging one day, and Cam asked him if he was sleeping at night. Tim informed him not very well, because he had no bed, and then shared some details of the living conditions within his house. Cam went home that night and told his mom that she needed to do something about what Tim had to endure. Cam's mom was reluctant to get involved and refrained from doing anything at the time. Later the same day, Cam asked his mom again if she had done anything and told her he would not be going to bed that evening until she had made a call to see about getting something done about Tim's situation. That call to a community member eventually placed Tim in the custody of new guardians, and he now had a bed, clothes, and food, and never again went without. The rest of the year Tim not only attended every practice, but he jumped in every drill, every time we needed someone on special teams, or scout team, he was one of the first to volunteer. There were times I had to take him out to put in someone who was a little bigger or faster to give our first team the look they needed. But Tim never complained.

At one point during the year Cam had been frustrated with his teammates and had gotten on them pretty hard. On the way home Tim took the opportunity to humble the Team Captain with his own explanation of how he should never address his teammates in that manner again if he truly wanted them to play for him. It was now Tim who was giving back to Cam. Tim played some offense, defense, and special teams in freshman games, JV games; and in one varsity game, Tim recorded his one and only tackle. Tim also improved himself in the classroom.

Tim has been accepted by two universities for the fall semester and will have his choice in where to attend. At the end of the year the team votes on a sheet of paper for team awards, and there is a place to write thoughts on the year, good or bad, that you may have. It was late and I thought everyone had cleared out of the locker room, not Tim --- he had written under the question, turned the paper over and had almost filled the back page. The following text is what Tim wrote that day; this was later engraved on two plaques, one that was given to him and a second that hangs in our locker room, so that others can see what this game we all love and endure is all about.

BURG FOOTBALL

"Football changed my life in its entirety. I was not in a position in my life to succeed or excel.

I asked on a paper in the beginning that football would provide for me an environment that promoted hard work, respect and success. I gained from this year far more than I had asked. I am now in a position to succeed and excel in my life. I have an opportunity to go to college, a better home life, a more determined work ethic, and moral values, all of which I can attribute to this wonderful football program and the people associated with it, whether that be the coaches, my teammates, or the community. I cannot in words describe how thankful I am for the opportunity to play and be a part of the team. I cannot thank the program enough for the life lessons I have learned. I've learned football is a game of winning and losing. Not just the game, but everything you win and learn in the process. Individually every player wins the respect of his teammates and his coaches. With that we've won their friendships and the right to call each other brothers and family. As a team we've won the respect of the community and our opponents. My father always told me the secret to happiness is to find something more important than yourself and dedicate your life to it. I never understood what he meant by that until I became part of this team and learned what it means to dedicate your life to your family, and your community."

TIM ADKINS - # 61 – DT
One Varsity Tackle & a Lifetime of Memories

COURAGE, COMMITMENT, DETERMINATION

In the fall of 1988, I was the head football coach at Bishop Foley HS (Michigan). That season, I was out watching an 8th grade CYO football game and, in particular, watching an 8th grade player whose brother was on my varsity team.

The name of the 8th grade player was Troy Z. He came up to me after the game and told me that in 9th grade, he was going to be the starting center on my varsity team. His enthusiasm and optimism were contagious, even though I remember thinking that it was somewhat misguided.

During the spring of Troy's 8th grade year, an examination found that he had a heart problem and that open heart surgery was going to be performed during the summer before he enrolled in high school. At that time, I had given up any thought of Troy being able to play football again. The most important goal to reach was for him to be healthy and lead a normal life.

During the school year, I had lunch room supervision and I would see Troy and talk with him quite a bit. During the fall of his freshman year, you could see that he was down because he couldn't play football, so we would talk about everything positive going on in his life. The thought of him ever playing football again never crossed my mind. The surgical scar ran the length of his chest.

During the spring of Troy's sophomore year, again in lunch hour, Troy came up to tell me that he was playing football in the fall. I stood there, chuckled, and humored him, all the time thinking, "Yeah, right."

In August 1990, Troy and his dad came to a summer workout with paperwork that stated that Troy was cleared to play football. Along with myself, the coaching staff was astounded. What do we do? What do we say? Keep in mind, those were the days when high school coaches were the "trainers" on site.

During that preseason, all the coaches held their collective breath every time Troy ran, let alone going through drills. Coaches' faces were white every time Troy was slow to get up. Troy was an excellent long snapper, one of the best I have ever coached in 43 years of coaching football. The staff figured, what harm would it do in letting him snap on PATs and punts on the JV squad. Two or three games into the season, we realized that he was the best long snapper in the program, so we moved him up to the varsity to long snap only. In practice, he would take reps as offensive center, but we monitored him closely, again, holding our collective breath on every scrimmage down in practice. During the 6th game of the season, our starting center was injured and Troy jumped in and played the remainder of the game, while a worried coaching staff stood on the sidelines. Troy finished the game with a + rating and started the next game for us.

After finishing the first game he had ever started at the varsity level, Troy came up to me and apologized. I said, "For what?" He said that he was sorry he didn't start as a 9th grader for me and for letting me down because he had been "delayed" by circumstances in fulfilling his promise. All I remember at that moment were the tears in my eyes that were flowing before he had finished speaking.

In this story of courage, determination, and commitment, there is a fairy tale ending. During the next two seasons, Troy went on to earn First Team All Catholic Honors both years and ended up playing at a D-111 school and earned his degree.

When things are tough for me, I often think of Troy and his indomitable spirit, determination, and courage. He was an inspiration for an entire staff, team, and school community.

ED MALONEY

RAMBO

In my 14 years of coaching college football I have come across many student-athletes that have impacted my life, many of which have changed my approach to coaching. However, one player stands out as the most inspirational player I have come across.

It was while I was a young coach at Thomas More College that I met Brandon Ramey. I first met Brandon while I was giving a campus tour to some of the recruits we had on campus that day. While showing off the new dorms, Brandon was on a general admissions tour, which happened to be in the new dorms at the same time.

I won't ever forget our initial meeting because Brandon is not a kid that is easy to forget. Brandon stands out and it isn't because of his skin color, his height, or his weight. Brandon has cerebral palsy. He was born with CP, a disability that robs most kids of a normal life. He has a lot of trouble with his speech and can be tough to understand when you first meet him. He also has some motor skill deficiencies that make it tough for him move around comfortably.

On this day, he walked right up to me and introduced himself and his intentions to play college football at Thomas More next year. Being a young coach, I was not sure how to handle this situation. I bought myself a little time by telling him to come see me in the cafeteria at lunch where I would have some time to talk to him. I ran the situation by our Head Coach at the time, Dean Paul. Coach Paul was extremely supportive of the idea of accepting Brandon into our program. We weren't sure if he would be able to participate as a member of our team due to his physical limitations, but we felt that if he couldn't get cleared by his doctors or our training staff, at least we could make him a student-coach or a team manager.

It was at lunch that I learned all I needed to know about Brandon. I brought a questionnaire for him to fill out. As he tried to write his name and address on the questionnaire I could see that he struggled to hold a pen and his handwriting was extremely slow and illegible. I offered to write the information for him, but he refused the help and was adamant that he could do it himself. Our conversation at lunch was a long one, partly because I was intrigued by his situation and partly because I had a hard time understanding him, so I had to ask him to repeat things quite often.

Brandon left a tremendous impact on our entire coaching staff that day and we were anxious to have him join our team in whatever capacity would work the best. As August approached, Brandon was cleared by all medical personnel and he was an active member of our incoming recruiting class.

It didn't take long for Brandon, whom our players referred to as "Rambo", to stand out. It was not because of his CP though. Early in camp we liked to have our upperclassmen take a shot at correctly naming as many of the incoming freshman as possible. We would let three or four guys give it a shot before we started our team meetings. We had a class of roughly 85 freshman, so it was not an easy chore. Most of the upperclassmen couldn't get half of the names correct. On the second day of attempting this, Rambo asked if he could give it a try. Brandon went on to not only correctly name nearly every freshman, but then he went on to name all of the upperclassmen as well.

On the field is where his disabilities were too big of a hindrance for his enormous passion for the game of football to overcome. On testing day, Rambo ran the 40, but it was painful to watch. He fell down several times attempting the pro-agility shuttle run. In the weight room, he made all our coaches nervous as he attempted to bench, squat, and hang clean. Although none of his times or lifts were anything very impressive, the effort and intensity with which he performed these things was something that all our other players noticed.

Rambo never at any point used CP as an excuse to miss a 6am lift or to get out of conditioning drills. In fact, he became a vocal leader pushing other freshman to work a little harder. Brandon went to every position meeting, defensive meeting, and every special teams meeting fully preparing himself to play. I don't believe he ever entertained the thought that he could not be successful on the football field.

We selected a Players Committee made up of about four members of each class. This Committee was voted on by the players. Rambo was a unanimous selection to represent our freshman class on that committee. He wasn't selected because the players felt bad for him, he was selected because each and every member of our team respected his work ethic and passion.

I wish the story ended with Brandon overcoming all the odds and turning into a great football player, but that never happened. Physically, CP created too many limitations to his movement. However, Brandon was a captain of our JV team and handled himself well during those games.

As coaches, we want each player to reach their full potential. And time and time again we see gifted athletes that do not possess the passion and work ethic to become the best they can be. I know for sure that Rambo, more than anybody I have ever coached, reached his full potential.

Too often we measure our success as coaches only by how productive our players are on game day. Thanks to Rambo, I have learned that there are other responsibilities in coaching that will never show up on a stat sheet. Rambo had a successful playing career. He never started a game or made a big play. What he did as far as giving his heart, body, and soul to the game of football without the reward of playing time inspired all who played alongside him. He also impacted each one of our coaches on that staff and changed our approach to coaching in the process.

I still stay in contact with Rambo, who now has a full time job with The Castellini Company in the Cincinnati area. I hope he reads this book someday and can take a lot of pride in knowing that what he did mattered to a lot of people. And his example of courage, passion, and work ethic have directly influenced my philosophies as a coach. I want him to know that his sacrifices not only impacted the players that played with him but will continue to show up in the young men I coach in the future.

NOTE:

- Cerebral palsy, also known as CP, is a condition caused by injury to the parts of the brain that control the ability to use muscles. Cerebral means having to do with the brain. Palsy means weakness or problems with using the muscles. Often the injury happens before birth, sometimes during delivery or, in some cases, soon after birth. CP can be mild, moderate or severe. Brandon's case was mild.

- About 500,000 people in America have some form of CP. Each year, 8,000 infants and almost 1,500 preschool-age children are diagnosed with CP.

- With early and ongoing treatment, the effects of CP can be reduced.

- New medical treatments are being developed all the time. Sometimes surgery, Botox injections, or other medications can help lessen the effects of CP, but there is no cure for the condition.

SOURCE: National Information Center for Children and Youth with Disabilities.

BYRAN MOORE

DANNY

I had a promising freshman pitcher named Danny Goss, who absolutely loved the game. On the baseball field he threw pretty hard for a 15-year-old, and he earned a few appearances for our varsity at Bethel HS. His baseball future looked good until midsummer. Danny went to the doctor believing he had asthma. He was struggling getting his breath while attending a summer basketball camp. The doctor ran some tests and the x-rays discovered he had a large baseball-sized mass in front of his heart, and that he had Hodgkin's disease. Over the next two years, Danny suffered through surgeries, chemo, radiation treatments and complications. Things got so bad for his family that they lost their car and were financially broke. Danny was struggling and it appeared that he may not make it. His father told me that Danny would talk daily about how he intended to get better and come back and play baseball again. Every time I'd visit him in the hospital, we'd talk about baseball.

In the summer, when things looked the bleakest, I asked Jeff Greene, a former player who at that time was playing for the Atlanta Braves, to go with me to visit Danny. Jeff was home for a few days, as he was being promoted to the Durham Bulls. (Later that year, he was asked to be an extra in the movie *Bull Durham*, starring Kevin Cosner and Susan Sarandon.) Jeff brought a Braves hat, plus a spring training Braves shirt. I brought along one of my special Mickey Mantle ball cards to give to Danny. When we got there, the Goss family was told that Danny had to be moved to Louisville's Humana Hospital for some experimental type of radiation treatment, and things were worse. Danny's color was ash gray and it was all he could do to respond to Jeff and I. When Danny slipped off to sleep, Jeff and I left. It was so heart wrenching that Jeff had tears in his eyes, for a boy he'd only met once. Danny was supposed to be a junior that next fall, but had not gone to school in a year.

In the fall, the experimental treatment started to work and Danny slowly gained strength. He started back to school in January and began trying to catch up. His strength went up and down, and although he wanted to try to play he wasn't ready. During his junior year he was able to make up all of his classes for both his sophomore and junior years. Going into his senior year, Danny was honored by ESPN by winning the Arete Award for Courage. The show was broadcast from Chicago on Christmas morning, and Danny (dressed in a tuxedo) was given the award on national TV by Olympic star Mary Lou Reton. I was asked to do a guest shot that was filmed at the baseball field in early December, just after a major snowstorm. Boy was it cold, and we had to do six retakes because of extraneous sounds from nearby airplanes, garbage trucks, and kids playing on the playground nearby.

Everything seemed to be looking up, but Danny knew he had one more thing to conquer. Coming back to pitch his senior year: who knew? Would the strain be too great, the surgery to his chest too much to overcome? Baseball conditioning started in late January, and of course we adjusted his workload. We started to throw in February, and it was slow process, as a simple cold sometimes meant taking off 4 or 5 days to recover. As March began, it looked like Danny could pitch, if I picked the right opponent and was careful as to the pitch count and the weather.

Opening day, I decided Danny was going to be the starting pitcher. He'd paid a heavy price over the past three years, and he deserved the opportunity. We were all behind him that day. He pitched 5 innings, threw 92 pitches and our team won. No scouts were in attendance, it wasn't broadcast on TV, it wasn't a World Series or an "all-star game." There were no trophies or championships to be won but something bigger took place. I once told Cincinnati Reds owner Marge Schott that major league baseball doesn't own the game of baseball because I once was a little part of one of the most important games ever played. Watching Danny Goss step up to the mound truly was one of the biggest moments in baseball. No, the pros weren't playing, no records were broken, but it was still ranks as one of baseball's best games ever. Baseball inspired a boy's desire so much that he faced death, and endured life-threatening surgery and experimental radiation therapy, to overcome huge obstacles just to play the game one more time. In today's amateur baseball world, so involved with showcases, camps, being recruited, draft picks, scholarships, and money, I'll always think of Danny Goss, who forever symbolizes for me the real "love of the game."

COACH FROSTY BROWN

SACRIFICE!

Every day Big Bill would get up at 4 am and deliver 150 newspapers. It would take him about two hours on his Schwinn bicycle. Rain or snow. The Tennessee weather was unpredictable, but he never missed a day his last three years of football. His day was just beginning.

He would get home around 6:30 am, and get breakfast ready for his two younger brothers. He would then walk them to the bus stop and get them on Bus #2, then he would walk three blocks and take a city bus to his school.

His mother worked part-time until 10:00 am at FedEx as a janitor, so Big Bill, as he was called, had to be the father figure. Bill's father had never been around, so all Bill did was manage the normal, needed routine.

His school day was somewhat normal. But the fact that he was a B student was a testament to his discipline and hard work despite all his extra duties. He would go to practice and be one of the hardest workers on the team. As an offensive lineman he helped lead a very productive offense, and was a team captain his senior year.

Each day when he got home his mom was ready to go to bed, so he would make his brothers dinner, make sure they did their homework, and get them in bed by 9:00. Then he cleaned the kitchen and got his homework done. In the summer he worked at the Dixie Ice Cream Shop. He would often refer to himself as Big Bill. He got a laugh from his teammates when he said Big Bill likes ice cream!

The coaches did not know that this was Big Bill's routine until his junior year, when the team had a team-building function. The theme was what can you do to make sacrifices for this year's team. Each player was asked what sacrifices they did --- what they did at home for their family. When Big Bill spoke, he stood up and rattled off his daily schedule. His schedule, his personal daily sacrifices, were much more intense and busier than any of his teammates.

When Big Bill was asked to define sacrifice, his answer was amazingly simple. He said, after thinking about it briefly: Sacrifice is just doing what needs to be done to get the job done and to help each other. As coaches, we were shocked at the simplicity and clarity of how well Big Bill understood sacrifice. Bill went on to Memphis University, graduated, and is now a physical therapist. He continues to serve.

Big Bill got the Most Inspirational Player award as a senior. The best part of Big Bill was that, in his heart, he felt what he did was normal. Well, it is not and as a coach his dedication and personal sacrifices for his family and his team really inspired us all to give a little more!

COACH D.

THE JOURNEY

My first year as a head football coach was 1976, so I believe I am entering my 46th year in that position. My first five years were at my alma mater, Trotwood Madison, then I spent seven years at Archbishop Alter, eleven years at Northmont, and then back to Alter from 1999 to the present (2021).

I suppose like so many others, I have relished the journey and the many relationships developed over the years. I have been blessed with loyal, dedicated assistant coaches who have shouldered much of the coaching responsibilities. It has also been my pleasure to have coached some remarkable young men. Yes, some of these possessed amazing skills, but I am also referring to the many who were not necessarily gifted athletes but fine, hardworking young men. I have often said that my favorite players are the hardest workers, regardless of their talent.

Our teams have been fortunate to win many games over those 46 years. But we have also had to cope with disappointing results. Twice I have experienced 0-10 seasons. One of these was my 16th season. We had some great kids ... just not enough of them. My other 0-10 was my first year at Trotwood. I made a lot of mistakes, as most 26-year-old head coaches might. Year Two wasn't much better, as we finished 2-8. That 1977 season they ran a picture of the victory bell in the local paper with the caption "Will it ever ring again?" We won that week.

I would like to share a memory from 2008. We had an excellent team at Alter that year. We won our first three games and this looked to be one of the best teams in school history. We found out during week four that one of our seniors, a first year player, was in his fifth year of high school. He had transferred to Alter his freshman year and our principal had agreed to allow him to retake his ninth grade year. We, of course, had no knowledge of this arrangement. The young man decided to play football his senior year and got in the game for two or three plays at the end of our first two games.

When a counselor brought it to my attention that this was his fifth year in high school, I knew we were in trouble. Right away I checked with our athletic director Chris Hart. Honestly, I asked if there was any possible way that we might be able to avoid forfeiting those first two games. There was nothing we could find in the rules that offered any hope. We contacted the OHSAA and subsequently they ruled as we felt they would...we would be required to forfeit the first two games.

The most remarkable part of the story came afterwards. Our kids never blamed the young man for the loss of the two games. The team never broke stride. We finished the season without a loss on the field and defeated Steubenville in the State Championship game. What a tribute to those kids!

I learned a lot those first few seasons at Trotwood. I came to understand the importance of organization, allowing your coaches to coach and that the best coaches were also great teachers.

I knew from my junior year in high school that I wanted to coach football and teach Social Studies, and I have been able to live out that dream. I can't imagine a more rewarding vocation.

ED DOMSITZ

FOOTBALL IS MORE THAN JUST A GAME, SPORT, OR A SINGLE LESSON...

Football is where a boy can become a man ... right Jim!

Football is where someone can prove all the doubters wrong ... right Woody!

Football is where character is revealed to the world ... right Donny!

Football is where young men find a stage to compete in pure joy ... right Kaleb!

Football is where the little guy ends his career with the game of his life against the state champs ... right Alex!

Football is where many kids find the courage and motivation to join the military ... right Caleb, Jakob, Cody, Frank, Chayse, Cannon, Tyler, and many, many more!

Football is where your physicality and toughness are welcome ... right Lee!

Football is where being on the kickoff team every Friday night makes you one of the guys ... right Cody!

Football is where moving from RB to Guard becomes the most fun move ever ... right Grant!

Football is where all your hard work and fighting spirit might just save your life ... right John!

Football is where we learn that love is sacrifice and without love there is no team ... right Mike!

Football is where boys find a family to belong to ... right TEAMS everywhere!

Football is where representing your school, town, and community is a privilege and responsibility that is welcomed with open arms ... right TEAMS everywhere!

Football is where people of all shapes, sizes, and backgrounds come together to achieve a common goal ... of being a TEAM!

Fight On! Go Burg!

KURT FORREST

WE > ME...

It seems since the beginning of time, or in this case, since I began playing football in the 4th grade: every coach I ever had compared "life to football" at some point during the season. But to be honest, I could not remember one time where this comparison would be validated. After 35 years of coaching, I'm sure I was guilty on more than one occasion of using this analogy on my players. But I'll never forget two instances over the course of being a head coach for 21 seasons that this phenomenon unfolded before my eyes without any prompting.

The first occurrence happened with a young man named Colin. Colin and my youngest son, Michael, were classmates, thus making this situation a little more sensitive --- actually, a lot more sensitive. Colin played linebacker from his time during youth football, through junior high school, and up until his senior year in high school. Because Colin was growing at an incredible rate, he basically grew out of his dream --- to play middle linebacker for his team as a senior.

Colin now stood 6'4" and weighed in at about 230 lbs. He was simply too slow for that position by now. Not to mention, we had younger players who were better than him. My conversation with him was difficult but necessary. I gave Colin the option of staying at linebacker and possibly playing as a backup or moving to the last under-appreciated and most overlooked position in football --- the offensive line. As tears rolled down his face and reality began to set in, I gave him the weekend to think about what he wanted to do and to give me his answer on Monday.

When I saw Colin on Monday, he informed me that he would move to the offense line. While this was a relief for me to hear his decision, the move to that position group and to carry a bad attitude could impact our team profoundly since he was a senior that was respected and well liked by everyone on the team. In the coming weeks, Colin settled in at the guard position.

By the season's end, Colin would be our best lineman on a team that ended up being conference champions and made it to the quarter finals of the playoffs. Colin went one to earn first team all conference, Most

Improved Player of the Year, and All District. Had he chosen to stay at linebacker, he would have experienced none of these things.

Although Colin chose not to play football in college, he did choose to study law, and now has his own successful law firm. I'm confident that Colin will never forget the day he and I had that very hard conversation. I am also confident that he'll remember the choice he made was for his team and not himself.

The second time where "football turned life" was with a young man named Blake. It happened at the onset of Blake's junior season. At that time, he stood 6'4" and weighed in at about 200 lbs (soaking wet!). He had "a motor" like none I've ever seen in a player. It was like he never got tired, regardless of what we were doing. He always finished first in his position group during conditioning. His competitive spirit was raging 24/7!

I had been dreading this conversation for almost a year. When you're the head coach, you always tried to make sure you never "stockpiled" too many great players at the same position. It was always a priority for me to play the best 11 players! Blake wanted to play outside linebacker. And he was very good at it. Once again, we had one of my better teams returning for that season. The problem was we had both outside linebackers returning, and both were all conference a year ago!

Prior to meeting with Blake, I ran through my mind how I thought our meeting would go. Not once did I see it being easy or comfortable for either of us. In fact, I anticipated Blake wanting to compete to beat either of them out. The truth is, he probably could have. But what I was wanting Blake to do, neither of those all conference outside linebackers could do. And that was to put their hand in the dirt and play the defensive line. So when I shared his options of rotating in at OLB and playing 1/3 of the snaps, or playing defensive tackle, his answer was simply overwhelming to me as a head coach. His response, "Coach, I don't care where I play, I just want to play!"

As a junior defensive lineman at 6'4" 200 lbs, and who ran about a 4.7/40, Blake registered a school record: 18 sacks as a junior! We were conference champions, state ranked, and finished 12-1, losing in the regional final to the eventual state champ. As for Blake, he was 1st team all conference, all city, and a finalist for Defensive Player of the Year in our conference. Blake went on to have another solid season at defensive tackle, as we were once again conference champions, and he led our defense as a captain. Blake's choice to put the team first earned him several accolades. This would include a full-ride D1 athletic scholarship to play football at the position of … outside linebacker!

ANDY OLDS

COACHING: A WILD RIDE

As I eagerly awaited the start of my senior year at the University of Dayton, I was filled with excitement and hope. My first three seasons as a Flyer did not go as planned. From being at the bottom of the depth chart, to a long list of injuries, I found myself ready to prove not only to myself, but to everyone around me that I could be a contributor on the field.

Fall has arrived, and I find myself in a starting role, ready to take my first meaningful snaps as a college athlete. Little did I know, this season was going to be the hardest and most challenging time in my life. After our second game vs. Robert Morris, I noticed an odd and unusual feeling in my right foot. I went into practice that week with the mentality that the pain would go away, and I would be ready to go for Saturday. That was not the case; the pain got progressively worse, and the seriousness of this injury was setting in. Our team doctor ordered me to get an MRI and the results showed that I had suffered a high-degree stress fracture in my right foot, sidelining me for 4 weeks.

When I first heard the news, I did not know what to think. I kept asking myself, why me? This season was supposed to be my opportunity, my chance to play the game I had worked so desperately hard for. I knew there was only one option, and that was to hold on to that same excitement and hope I had prior to the start of the season. With hard work and perseverance, I was able to come back more quickly than anticipated and was cleared to play the final four games.

As every college athlete knows, this game is a business, and winning is everything. My first game back from injury I played a grand total of three plays. I started to feel discouraged and frustrated with my playing time. My relationship with my Wide Receiver Coach had begun to diminish and I began to feel forgotten. Next week rolls around, and the narrative stays the same. My approach to and mentality in the game were at an all-time low. I wanted nothing to do with football; I was checked out. After everything I went through to come back, not seeing the field as a senior was the hardest pill I have ever had to swallow. I will never forget seeing my dad after one of our home games. He looked at me and was overwhelmed with emotion, expressing how sorry he felt for the situation

I was in. Seeing my dad cry that day was one of the saddest moments in my life. This was not at all how I envisioned my last chapter as a football player. A game that I had been playing since I was six years old was not supposed to end like this. In the blink of an eye, my football career was over, and I was left with a hole in my heart.

For as long as I could remember, being a football coach was all I ever wanted to do. I still remember those talks I would have with my parents at the kitchen table, talking endlessly about how this dream would one day turn into a reality. After my senior year concluded, my focus and attention were solely set on chasing this goal; however, I found myself more driven than ever. I was not going to let my experience as a player hold me back from being the coach I know I was destined to be. Instead, I was going to use my past failures and obstacles as motivation to achieve and aspire to be my best self. See, the game of the football works in mysterious ways. The life lessons that this game can teach us go above and beyond our expectations. During my time at Dayton, I did everything the right way. I worked as hard as I could, was a team player, treated everyone with respect, and carried myself to a higher standard. With that said, I was not meant to reap the benefits and accomplishments on the field as a player; I was destined for something different.

The life of a coach is nothing short of ordinary. It has been one calendar year since I have ventured into this crazy, wild, and unexpected life. During this time, I have held 3 different jobs in 3 different states. It may sound crazy, but I would not change a damn thing. As a young coach, I have been so blessed to be surrounded by great-minded coaches, but more importantly by great people. Along with that, I have been supported from the very beginning by my family and without them this dream holds no existence. Throughout this year I have seen myself grow in so many ways, whether that be professionally or personally. The lifestyle of a coach is an extreme sacrifice that affects not only yourself, but those around you. I am so blessed to have crossed paths with so many amazing people in such a short amount of time. If you ask me, life is all about experiences and relationships. I would not trade this past year for anything; I truly am living a childhood dream.

I am forever grateful for the journey the game of football has brought me on. During this time, I have faced many difficult and challenging situations, not knowing at the time, but these experiences have molded me into the coach I am today.

Looking back at my experience at Dayton, I lost sight of what truly was important. I let my emotions and pride get the best of me, ultimately steering me away from the love I have for the game. Going to the University of Dayton was the best decision I have ever made. Not because of what transpired on the field; rather, I was able to grow and become a better man in the process. The journey I went through my senior year showed me a different perspective, not only in football, but in life. Many of us believe if we work hard at something, it is guaranteed that we will succeed. In reality, nothing in this life is given, and we are all limited in our opportunities to live out our dream. It may sound ridiculous, but I am so thankful for every hurdle that was thrown my way. I never achieved anything close to what I wanted to as a player, but my life in football is just getting started. As I previously said, the game of football works in mysterious ways. Never did I imagine I would go to school in Ohio or end up coaching in Illinois or Indiana, but this is the journey I am living. I really consider myself the luckiest man in the world. Each day I have the opportunity to chase a dream that keeps me hungry and excited for more.

I am proud to say I am shaped by the game of football, and I am so excited to see where this journey goes.

SAM COSTANTINO

A HALLOWEEN MIRACLE

In 2008, we took over a program that was 0-36. Four years later, we finished the season 8-2 and made the State Playoffs for the first time ever, capping the greatest season in school history. The following year, we struggled with injury and inconsistent play. That year, on October 31st, Halloween night, we played our conference rival, which our team had never beaten. Because of our success the prior year, we had gained a lot of media attention, including a few games being televised on local TV. The game on Halloween night was one of those televised games.

The whole week I had emphasized to the staff that I did not want us to appear in any way sloppy, unorganized, and undisciplined: "I don't want to see anyone running on the field late for special teams!" etc.

Friday night comes and we feel like we've had a pretty good week of practice. Also that night, Halloween night, was a driving rainstorm. Anyhow, we lost the toss and the other team deferred to the 2nd half, so we received the opening kickoff and returned it close to our own 15 yd line. We called the opening on the sideline, so our offense trotted out for the first play. We line up and we aren't snapping the ball. Our QB is looking around confused, like he is unsure how to proceed. I started yelling, "Let's go!" "Run the play!" The QB starts yelling something to our sideline. Since I have a headset on, I can't hear him. I ask one of our assistant coaches what he is yelling and he proceeds to tell me, "Coach, we don't have a Center." "What the heck do you mean, we don't have a Center?!"

Well, we didn't have a Center on the field, so we had to call timeout on the first play of the game to get our 2nd team center in! Well, needless to say, the poor kid wasn't warned up and extremely nervous, and proceeds to snap the ball way left of our QB, all the way back to the 3 yd line, where the opposing team recovers. The next play they score and we're losing 7-0. So much for not looking sloppy and unorganized on local television!

As it turned out, our starting Center had broken his non-dominant wrist earlier in the season, but could still play with it casted. And play well he did. However, in pre-game, the officials deemed the tape job to be inefficient and he was sent back into the training room to have the cast retaped. He did tell the appropriate personnel that he had to go back inside, but that message was never relayed back to the coaching staff.

Wow! Just brutal! What a miserable feeling as a Head Coach to put on that display. However, we went on to dominate the rest of the game and won by a score of 35-14, beating them for the first time ever! Turned out to be a pretty good game and a great Halloween night!

GEORGE KONTSIS
Former Head Football Coach
Walnut Hills High School
Cincinnati, Ohio

THE WINNING ATTITUDE

It is interesting to note how the attitude of a football team shapes the success of the season. I have been on teams in the past where the attitudes of the players just feel different. When guys are totally locked in and committed, you feel that energy. When it seems like the team is not doing everything to be successful, you feel that too. When you have been a part of a championship team and season, you get to know and understand what success feels like. After this, you can get a pretty good idea of how the season is going to go based on the attitudes of the guys on the team. Winning a championship, in theory, lays out a blueprint for success for years to come. If this is true, however, then why is it so rare for teams to win back-to-back championships? I would say it is because the players' attitudes truly drive a team's success. It is easy to recreate practices, offseason training routines, film study times, and more, but it is not easy to recreate the commitment, drive, and winning attitude of a remarkable team.

So, we have established that successful teams are driven by the attitudes of their players. The question is, how can those attitudes be coached or developed? The answer is simple: they cannot. Motivation comes from within, and no matter how hard a coach or teammate tries to push someone to do something they do not want to do, the result will never be achieved until the person decides to take up the challenge on his own. This is why it is imperative for college coaches to recruit talent AND character instead of talent alone. When you understand this, it makes winning a championship even more impressive. When you think about it, you must have a perfect combination of successful recruiting, physical development, buy-in/winning attitude from players, proper game-planning and management, and the right amount of luck (star QB staying healthy, etc.). It takes a group of special players to understand this challenge, choose to accept it despite its difficulty, and stay committed to the end goal for an entire season. When this happens, you win a championship.

As a player, I was only part of one championship. This was my sophomore year of high school at Providence Catholic. The attitude of that team was certainly different than the attitudes of teams I was on that were not championship caliber. What made this team successful was the fact that it was a "player coached team". What I mean by this is that the coaches were never on us to give more effort, watch more film, spend more time in the weight room, and more. There was an overall desire from the team to win at all costs. There was nothing selfish about this team either. Guys wanted everyone to get better and, as a "player coached team", our teammates corrected each other's mistakes with no motive other than to better the whole. Outside of college, I have never been a part of more intense weight room sessions, efficient practices, and intelligent football conversations then that championship season. The work we put in showed up on gameday. Our offense was electric, with receivers who could take the top off the defense, a quarterback smart enough to call plays at the line of scrimmage, a line with the will to protect the quarterback and make space for the ball carrier, and a hard-nosed running back (me). Our defense was fierce, made up of a line full of some of the best athletes on the team, a discipline linebacking core who knew every play a team could run against us, and a young group of defensive backs who were not afraid to come down hill and make a tackle. By the time the season was over, and we were holding the championship trophy, we were all brothers. Seven years later, we are still brothers. In fact, a core group of us keep in contact almost daily. It certainly was that perfect combination discussed earlier that led us to a championship season.

Now that we have discussed what a winning attitude does for a team, the idea that the winning attitude comes from within, and a personal example of the winning attitude at work, you are probably wondering what type of people carry this mindset and can foster it across an entire team. Well, I think it is no coincidence that seven players on my high school championship football team have gone on to serve in the United States Military. This includes one Navy SEAL and another currently in SEAL training. Pretty special, huh? I have always had a great admiration for the men and women in our military. My grandpa served in the Army and two of my uncles in the Marines. Growing up, it was easy to look up to them as role models of sacrifice, courage, and devotion. Furthermore, it seems like football is always likened to aspects of the military. We refer to games as battles, we prepare ourselves for the enemy's attack, we discipline ourselves through rigorous training both mentally and physically, and more. Just like in the military, we look to our leaders (captains) for guidance and direction. In my opinion, there is no better organization in which any team should model itself after in terms of core values, training, and being part of something bigger than yourself.

It makes me proud to know that I played alongside seven individuals who now serve alongside other Americans who are willing to risk their lives to keep people like you and me safe. We committed to the challenge and discipline of a high school football season, and now they have committed to the challenge of protecting this country. These are the people who fostered the winning attitude on my high school team. Now, they have taken it to the next level. I will never forget the lessons I learned from these individuals, and I continue to learn from them today. I owe much of my success in college to these individuals as well. When things got challenging, when I was fatigued, when I struggled mentally, when I could not seem to grasp a concept, I would think about my seven high school teammates and what they could possibly be doing during that moment. Putting things into perspective is a powerful thing to do. It makes you realize how small your problems are compared to those of others in the world. In these moments, I thought to myself, "If they can make it through SEAL training, I can finish this last sprint," or "If he can jump out of an airplane into battle, I can block this linebacker." This was not to diminish the work I was doing, but it was to understand that there are far more important challenges taken up by people across the world daily.

Hopefully, this short reflection and anecdote serves its intended purpose: to make you realize why some teams are successful and others are not, to show how hard it is to win a championship, to introduce you to the types of people who lead championship teams, and to understand how small our sacrifice to play football is compared to those willing to make the ultimate sacrifice. At the end of the day, a football team is about the players. If we treat our players like people who have something to teach us, then we may just learn something from them. If we can put ego aside and work for the betterment of others, then we can truly be a team. Finally, when the going gets tough, and you feel like you are ready to quit, think about someone in your life who has inspired you. Think about what it is that made you want to be like them. Think about what they would do in that situation and emulate it. When we do this, we become the example, we become the heartbeat of the team, and we have the winning attitude to lead it to a championship.

RICHIE WARFIELD
University of Dayton '21
4 Year Member of the Corp
2020 Special Forces Captain

MY VIEW ON "THE VIEW"

There are many ups and downs in the coaching profession; along with all the joys of wins and even of losses, what makes a coach want to pursue this profession? Before I get into some of the things we did at the "View," I must give an answer to: why coach? For me it was a simple answer: I wanted to chase the profession when I was still in high school. I love football! I grew up in Greenville, Ohio. I am a Darke County farm kid. I was part of a great tradition for the Wave; back in the mid-1970s, we were 37-3 for the Wave. I was fortunate enough to play for Wilmington College, where we never experienced a losing season in the 4 years I was there. I was fortunate to play for Coach Tom Holman at Greenville and legendary Coach Bill Ramseyer at Wilmington.

Along the way these coaches, and teachers and professors, and the Greatest Game, help give me the ultimate platform to serve and teach. You know at graduations (both in high school and college) you hear all these speeches and wonder if you could give something to someone, and that they might become something they thought could never become. My high school and college experiences helped shape what I wanted to do as a coach. As a player I was extremely competitive; when you hang up your cleats and step away from the game, what do you do with that competitive fire? Coach!

At Wilmington, my interaction with the Bengals and some of their staff and players put me in the path of what I wanted to do: coach. I started my career in 1979, at Watkins Memorial High School. Coaching there, our one-year highlight was a 7-6 victory over traditional State Champ Newark Catholic. The QB I worked with had an outstanding career at Toledo and pitched for the Orioles. I became a head coach the following year at a well-known powerhouse (at the time of this writing): Clinton Massie High School. SO... I had 52 boys at Massie for the meeting ... which was awesome as they only had 70 boys in the whole school. I inherited a 0-40 team. Here I was, this young guy "full of piss and vinegar," probably the youngest head high school coach in Ohio... I thought I had a lot of ideas about coaching. We only had 20 players come out and finished the season late with a 1-9 record. However, that 1-9 season, on the bus ride back, you would have thought those players won the Super Bowl. The following season we had 51 boys ... some of those kids had never heard a halftime speech or adjustment, as about a half-dozen of them marched in the band with their football uniforms on. I left Massie with a foundation they could build on.

I came to the "View" in 1984. If you are not familiar with Valley View, the school is a consolidation of Germantown High School and Farmersville High School, smack in the middle of a corn field between Germantown and Farmersville. Valley View was best known for producing Miss USA Kim Seelbrede in '81, and for Thomas Howard, who played 11 years in the MLB and was skilled in both football and baseball...Michigan offered him a scholarship and he passed, as they wouldn't let him play both baseball and football then, so he just was an All-MAC Player at Ball State in both. I had the opportunity at Carlisle to try to get our defense to defend him; we could not.

My first order of business after I was hired in late July was to put something in the paper to let kids/parents know of a football meeting. I went down to the local paper, The Germantown Press, introduced myself, and gave them what I wanted printed for an announcement. I told the folks there, at the time, that we would put this place on the map: that was my vision. Well, the ladies of "The Press" gave me that look, as probably they thought I might have just gone to happy hour earlier at the nearby bar.

We had one sub .500 season in my first 6 years. We just couldn't get past Brookville as they dominated the SWBL in the mid-1980s. In 1989, one of our schools in the league could not pass a levy so we scrambled to find a game week 10. We had the option of playing Canton McKinley, Canton Central Catholic, or Portsmouth. We picked up Portsmouth. So, we loaded up the buses and drove down to the river, 124 miles on the big Yellow Birds. We gave them a game even though we did not match up with them. The week before the Trojans of Portsmouth fell to eventual State Champ CAPE (Cincinnati Academy of Physical Education), they had a running back you might recognize: Carlos Snow, who had played for OSU.

We were outgunned: they were huge, and fast, and it would have been ugly if we lined up in our conventional sets. Yes, we did lose, but with the loss laid the foundation, or should I say we put the footers in, for our future. During the bus ride back, I spoke to the coaches, as this was a 6-4 year, and told them we are putting in the Shoot, we are platooning our kids and we will line up on defense and play like our heads are on fire. I think one of the coaches said, calm down, we got 124 miles to get back to school; and think about it I did.

In 1990 we had just 33 players and we platooned: we were .500 that first year but the kids were like, I don't have to play both ways, I can play a position somewhere. In 1991 we went 8-2 and our numbers started going up. Then in 1992 and 1993, our numbers expanded; we went back-to-back 12-1 seasons, then we went undefeated in the SWBL, losing to Ironton both times in the Sate Semi. Our players numbered from 33 to about 73, then we had 80 plus players with our system.

The 1992 and 1993 teams set the table for the state title teams, yet were somewhat overshadowed by the state championships. Hopefully when this book goes to print, they will have their reckoning. Those teams were so dominant. We caught a lot of grief and even a few editorials about the scores of our games. They didn't have the mercy rule. Interesting now, you see big scores even with that rule. Few teams knew back then how to defend a one back offense.

We played our rival Brookville and there were two incidents that I recall. One was when we were signaling plays and I inadvertently pulled on my sleeve, I asked what we were running and my coach who signaled asked if I sent the play; I asked him, did you? The QB threw it for a big gain, and at the time the game wasn't decided. We gave our kids a lot of freedom on the field. Teams didn't know how to deal with motions and formations. "Get better or get bitter."

Another incident happened when one of our best linebackers intercepted a pass and celebrated his interception and score and with the Nestea plunge. Very much frowned on, but just a lot of emotion when you have been getting beat and lose out by the same team for years. Reading between the lines, you might think we lacked discipline. We let the kids have fun on Friday night. Things we did years ago you cannot do in this world we live in now, where everybody gets a trophy and if a voice is raised, you'll be called out on Facebook or Twitter.

We had a "Toast Board" on our locker room wall, if you got burnt on a pass play, your name went up. We also gave out the "Lunch Box" award: If you got knocked down or just smoked, you are carrying the lunch box to and from lunch and all your classes. If you fumbled, you might be carrying that ball with you all week and any student walking down the hall might hit it out. The times have changed, haven't they. We had the "Big Stick" award... you smoke someone, you get to carry the Big Stick around at school: a 2x4 that had a handle. All these things changed with the times.

We had a situation where we had a player that complained about not getting the ball thrown to him. His father was also a board member, so you can see there are politics in everything. This young man was terribly slow for our wide receivers. He could run a 5.6 or 5.5 40 yd dash on a good day. We had a significant lead in a game and had a time out. My QB came over and said let's put him in, so we did.

He ran a post route and the ball hit his hands and almost went to a defender. The next play we called for a quick hitch; my QB threw it and it almost got stuck in his face mask. The next play we ran an out cut and again he dropped it. The next play my QB called his own number and went in for a score. As we were coming off the field my QB said to me, "Coach, you're probably going to get called to the AD office to explain, because I just embarrassed that guy in front of 5,000 people."

Well, I didn't get called in, and the struggling young man in question became an outstanding attorney. My QB went on to play at Miami University and Southern Illinois. His dad cooled his jets and really became very thankful that we gave his kid a shot even though the young man didn't do so well. Later in the season we got him open for a huge gain.

In 1998 tragedy struck our team. We lost one of our outstanding linemen in a car wreck just a few hundred yards from our school. Our players were all very tight with this young man. Talk about an emotional roller coaster, after talking with this young man's parents they said to push on, so we did. I felt the emotions of all our players for the next few weeks.

I had never given a eulogy before. We lost a regional final game. The 39 games in a row winning streak was broken and that loss took its toll on a lot of folks.

I stated earlier that our community had high expectations. In 1994 we couldn't get the buses through town. That dwindled even though we won state titles in '96 and '97. In '97 we had just played the longest play-off game in Ohio football history: 5 overtimes. No parade. Things were just expected. Since 1998 so many teams had caught up with our mayhem. You could go to a clinic, and anyone can buy a video on the offense. Smaller schools are usually cyclical with their talent.

I could go on about some of the great teams and players we had, and we were still strong until the last season of 2011. We went to the regional finals several times. We had a 78-game winning streak at one time in our league. We played the longest game in Ohio history. We had a 39-game winning streak. We averaged 43.5 points a game for 11 years while only giving up 9.1. I'd say we might not have had the most talented players every year, but we had players that cared and fought every time they lined up on Friday night.

To summarize: Why coach? Because I love the game. You have a chance to help kids become something they think they cannot become. It's interesting that a lot of players stayed in our community to give back to the program, and even came back to the communities to raise their kids and keep the tradition that they built years before. They have immersed themselves in coaching their sons and daughters. There's something about raising kids in a small community where there is a great school that folks support!

That is my View and the memories that I will always cherish.

JAY NISWONGER
Former AD/Head Football Coach
Valley View "Spartan" Football

DANNY MAC!

It was a play like so many he had run since he was a young boy playing football in Troy, Ohio.

But this time he screamed and was laying on the practice field in pain, clutching his troublesome knee. He had been fighting with it for 2 years and he was losing. He was diagnosed with a torn ACL, and the knee just wouldn't hold up anymore. He needed surgery.

Troy has a long, storied football tradition; Dan McCormick was a tough, hard-nosed running back, like so many before him. He fought for every yard like it was the one that would win the game. He did that every snap he ever took. That is why I wanted him to play at Wittenberg University. He would be a solid Tiger. Dan had good speed and ran like a runaway rhino.

Early in his career he was behind some very talented running backs and worked hard to improve and always put the team first. He was a solid special teams (Rangers) performer. So his senior year he was going to be in the mix and be a big part of our offense as we chased a league title and a playoff berth. That's what made this so difficult. The knee injury pretty much spelled an end to his career.

Well, that's not how Dan saw it. "Mac" told me the next day that he was going to wait on surgery. He would wear a brace and build up the muscles around the knee. He was not going to abandon his brothers, per his words. He would do what he could and help the young guys. I explained to him and tried to convince him he could still make an impact and be on the team from the sideline. So, on he pushed doing everything he could. Every few days he would go down in a heap. But he would drag himself to his feet and keep showing up every day. His knee was pretty much bone on bone by now, but he wouldn't quit. He would bear the pain so he could be a leader on a championship team. He did that each day and we ended up getting a league championship. A huge part of that was Dan's inspirational toughness and grit!

His determination really spread in the running back room and across the team; guys saw his toughness each day just to be a great teammate.

Dan had surgery after the season and has gone on to a management role at FedEx. No doubt he has the same never-quit attitude as he leads his teammates at FedEx. In my 42 years of coaching, I never felt fighting through a knee injury, or any injury as serious as Dan had, is the way to go. But he was committed to the fight for his teammates, no matter what pain he would have to endure. It still amazes me and inspires me to fight through any adversity as it surfaces whenever I think of Danny Mac!

MTE

JOHNNY WILSON ("JW")

Like so many times before, I looked at the bill of my cap. For 41 of my 42 years of coaching, I often look at the bill of my cap, with the initials J.W. written there. It would often give me a sense of peace, sadness, and appreciation for the young man with wisdom well beyond his years.

This young man, at 9 years old, understood so much about the power of "team" and being an elite teammate. I was a junior in high school, chasing the starting QB job and volunteering at the local Catholic grade school coaching the St. Mark's Midget Football Team: 3rd, 4th and 5th graders. I became the *de facto* offensive coordinator by default. Our head coach was having health problems, so they turned to me to help call the game. I knew about 4 plays and even less about coaching. But I knew coaches had played an integral part in my life, especially when my father passed away when I was 12. I loved teaching the game and motivating kids, and I was enthusiastic and brought some "juice." That was about all I brought, and during the next few months my perspective of coaching changed, and I learned how a young man can also change your view of life.

Johnny was a 4th grader who was an invisible little guy. His shoulder pads went one direction and his helmet another when he ran. He was a dumpy little guy. Really did not have much skill, per se, but he loved being around his buddies and he was always talking. Always encouraging and kidding. Everyone got a kick out of the 9-year-old defensive tackle.

We did not really think much was wrong after he missed a Monday practice, and that extended into Tuesday. His teammates said he was not in school as well. We just figured he was sick and back then we didn't reach out. Wednesday was an off day. Thursday, we started practice and here comes Johnny. His grandparents were with him, along with Mom and Dad and lawn chairs.

Johnny comes right up to me as we stretched – him being late, I was ready to give him a hard time. But Johnny, in his confident way, stopped on a dime and turned towards me and some other coaches standing in front of the team and exclaimed, "I can't hit anybody, but I am going to work hard and be a part of the team." I always remember his focus and intensity. I looked over towards his parents and grandparents and smiled and they waved. Really did not think it was a big deal.

After practice, his parents and grandparents walked over towards me. When they arrived Johnny enthusiastically stepped in front and again said he would be at every practice and would be cheering his teammates along even if he could not hit. As I looked at him he was sad and confused but defiant. I assured him he was a part of this team. At that point, his grandpa spoke. He calmly said Johnny would not be able to play any contact sports until after they went to the Cleveland Clinic. He had gone to his family because of unusual bruising. They felt it might be a blood disorder. I did not say much other than, hang in there and let us know.

Johnny missed the next few practices, stretching into the next week and then missed a game. His constant chatter was really missed. He came back the next week and echoed the same sentiments – he barked, "I'll be here cheering my guys along!" And he did every day. Johnny was diagnosed with a very serious strain of leukemia. He would be back and forth to treatments, and it would be hit and miss at practice. Every time he did make practices, he was no different.

Barking, cheering, pushing his guys! He really relished being a great teammate. He was changing physically and seemed a bit slower. Before our second to last game, knowing he would be gone the next week in Cleveland for treatment, I asked him if he wanted to say anything. He didn't hesitate and stepped out in front of his team. He said this – "I love this team – We are gonna kick some butt this weekend. When I'm not with you I look at the clock and think about where you are in the game. I'm thinking of you guys and cheering you. We are the best team in our division. So go get a win!"

I was moved that a 9-year-old was giving a pep talk to us. And his young life was threatened.

One of his teammates said, "We love you Johnny!" We all came together and hugged and had a loud team cheer. Johnny's condition worsened and he missed the banquet two weeks later. He was awarded the Most Inspiring Player award. (He has been inspiring his former teammates and coaches for 40 years.)

I visited the Cleveland Clinic in late January, and everything had gone bad. He was so weak. His parents and grandparents were with him at all times. It was bad and it was so sad. It made you sick to your stomach. Johnny's breathing was slow and he couldn't say much but when I gave him the Inspirational Award, he beamed. You could see he was so proud! He whispered, "Tell the guys thanks!" Always thinking about his teammates!

Johnny passed away in late February, one month short of his 10th birthday. The funeral and the small casket were heartbreaking. All his teammates were there and it was such a moving day. Johnny had made a huge impression on all who crossed his young path. He loved being on a team, being a part of something that he loved. His fighting spirit is something that many adults years older never embrace. Johnny Wilson was a selfless winner!

He was the greatest teammate I have ever seen. His life, while being only 9 years, was a brilliant light that shines on in all the hearts who were blessed to know him.

Love You, J.W.
MTE

SHOW ME A HERO, AND I WILL WRITE YOU A TRAGEDY

As a leader, if we own the victories, do we not also have to own the defeats? If I told the story about the back-up Quarterback who led the last minute come-from-behind victory (against the hated arch-rival, no less), wouldn't I have to tell the story of the starter that drunkenly fell into a fire the previous Saturday? I could tell the story of the former players that attended a service academy, an Ivy league institution, or any highly selective school. I would also have to include that in every case these young men came from outstanding families, where their mothers and fathers were hardworking, honest, God fearing, and loving. But then would not I have to tell the tragic murder and/or suicide story. The perpetrators left behind hardworking, honest, God fearing, and loving parents who are left trying to answer unanswerable questions. I guess this is what is at the heart of Emerson's "Essay on Compensation" that Woody introduced me to so many years ago.

So do coaches make a real difference? I think they do. The best story I have is the one that I know best: mine. It is not an overwhelming story, probably underwhelming. I attended an "inner city" school in Akron. Of course, as a student I did not know it was "inner city" and all the negative stereotypes that go with the label. To me, it was school. Some kids had it together better than others. I guess I was a simpleton back then, too!

Our football teams won a few games and lost a whole lot of games. A whole lot. Somehow, even though a dense teenage male mind, I was able to see that Coach Peltz was able to maintain his dignity. He, more importantly, was able to make sure that we, as players, maintained ours. We would lose games, but never felt like losers. He never lost his belief in us or his confidence that good things were ahead. (Of course, he did lead the team to the playoffs... the year after I graduated!)

Understand, I did not come from a dysfunctional family. My parents loved me, and I knew it. There was discipline and expectation in the home. Granted, each parent had their own way of showing love and enforcing expectations. In hindsight, I believe that I would have made my way in the world, even if had not taken up football or sports at all.

So, how did Coach Peltz and football make such a big impact on my life? First, he reinforced the values taught in my home: work hard, get along with others, do what is best for the group, and welcome adversity. Secondly, his belief in me gave me confidence to explore opportunities to attend West Point, various Ivy league Schools, and other elite schools. Thirdly, I passed on those opportunities at higher institutions to become a teacher and coach. I believed then, and still believe today, that he provided hope and confidence to the kids who needed it. Some of my teammates grew up in tough situations. Coach provided those kids with the values I received at home. Having witnessed his influence, I thought I could best serve by attempting to provide that same hope and confidence to other young people.

While I struggle to grade myself on mentoring youth, I can testify to the power of coaches because of Coach Peltz. I greatly respect the coaches of the inner cities of this country. The frustrations of their positions are immense. Yet, they keep coming back and work to provide the hope and confidence that young people need. These coaches do not always have the best records, but to me they are "Coach of the Year" every year.

Coach Peltz is stepping down this year. Someone will be in his place next year. That man will do his best, as we all do. I hope that he can overcome the struggles and hardships and maintain his belief in making a difference. If he can do that, regardless of wins or loses, he is worthy of the Title: Coach.

COACH NEAL KASNER

PEANUT BUTTER & JELLY

During my 40+ years of coaching I have been blessed to witness so many success stories that have been life changing. I want to share one that shows how blessed we are to be a part of the game of football and how it can impact others.

In 2007 we had a young man named Guy that was our Team Manager. Guy had been classified as a special needs student and was limited in what he could do in a competitive athletic setting. He loved the game of football so much and was here every day, year round, just wanting to help. After two years, going into his senior year, he came to me and asked to become a player. It went from wearing a helmet during practice, until a few weeks later coming out of the equipment room in FULL PADS! I had long discussions with him for a couple of days, until we met with his parents. We came to an agreement that during certain parts of practice he could participate, under close observation from the staff. The rest of the team bought into this because of how he showed his excitement for the game of football.

We determined he would go with the defensive backs, which proved to be what was best for him. After a few weeks he improved, mostly because he had observed that group and understood the fundamentals. We taught him the coverage concepts as PEANUT BUTTER = sticky man and JELLY = loose zone. His dream to actually play in a game came true on senior night (our last regular season game). After discussion with parents, opposing coaches, officials, administration, and the state association, we decided to make it happen. We sent him in on the last series of defense and allowed him to actually get into a football game.

After the game the coaches, team, and fans gathered as they presented him the game ball. Guy continues to come by and visits with us, and has helped be a ball boy at some games after all these years.

EDDIE COURTNEY
Head Football Coach
Farragut HS
2016 Class 5A State Champions

Made in the USA
Monee, IL
14 May 2022